studysync®

Reading & Writing Companion
American Literature

UNIT 4

studysync.com

Send all inquiries to:
BookheadEd Learning, LLC
610 Daniel Young Drive
Sonoma, CA 95476

ISBN 978-1-97-016215-8

2 3 4 5 6 LMN 24 23 22 21 20

B

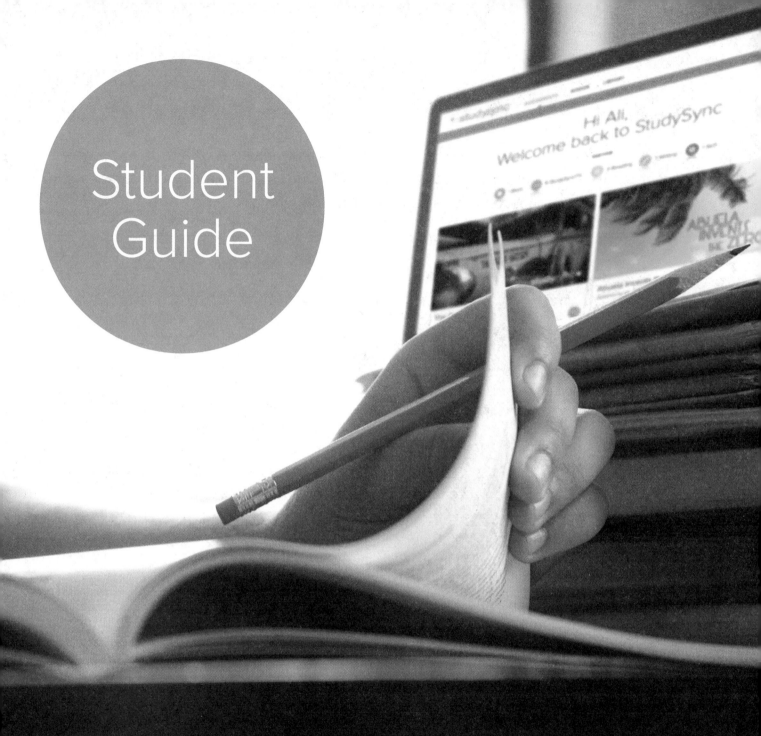

Student Guide

Getting Started

Welcome to the StudySync Reading & Writing Companion! In this book, you will find a collection of readings based on the literary focus of the unit you are studying. As you work through the readings, you will be asked to answer questions and perform a variety of tasks designed to help you closely analyze and understand each text selection. Read on for an explanation of each section of this book.

Close Reading and Writing Routine

In each unit, you will read texts and text excerpts that are from or are in some way connected to a particular period of American literature. Each reading encourages a closer look through questions and a short writing assignment.

Constitution of the Iroquois Nations

INFORMATIONAL TEXT
Dekanawidah (Oral Tradition)
Circa 1150

Introduction

Most information about Dekanawidah, co-founder of the Iroquois Confederacy, is lost to time. In Iroquois tradition, his name, meaning "two rivers flowing together," is used only under special circumstances. According to tradition, when the Iroquois tribes in present-day New York were torn apart by fighting, Dekanawidah stepped in to instill peace and unite the Iroquois nations. The oral constitution that followed represented an alliance among five tribes: the Seneca, Cayuga, Oneida, Onondaga, and Mohawk. A sixth tribe—the Tuscarora—later joined the union. Most historians believe that the democratic ideals of the Iroquois Constitution inspired the Constitution of the United States. The excerpt here includes about a dozen of the 117 total articles.

Constitution of the Iroquois Nations

"I am Dekanawidah and with the Five Nations' Confederate Lords I plant the Tree of Great Peace."

The Great Binding Law, Gayanashagowa

1. I am Dekanawidah and with the Five Nations' Confederate Lords I plant the Tree of Great Peace. I plant it in your territory, Adodarhoh, and the Onondaga Nation, in the territory of you who are Firekeepers.

I name the tree the Tree of the Great Long Leaves. Under the shade of this Tree of the Great Peace we spread the soft white feathery down of the globe thistle as seats for you, Adodarhoh, and your cousin Lords.

We place you upon those seats, spread soft with the feathery down of the globe thistle, there beneath the shade of the spreading branches of the Tree of Peace. There shall you sit and watch the Council Fire of the Confederacy of the Five Nations, and all the affairs of the Five Nations shall be transacted at this place before you, Adodarhoh, and your cousin Lords, by the Confederate Lords of the Five Nations.

2. Roots have spread out from the Tree of the Great Peace, one to the north, one to the east, one to the south and one to the west. The name of these roots is The Great White Roots and their nature is Peace and Strength.

If any man or any nation outside the Five Nations shall obey the laws of the Great Peace and make known their **disposition** to the Lords of the Confederacy, they may trace the Roots to the Tree and if their minds are clean and they are obedient and promise to obey the wishes of the Confederate Council, they shall be welcomed to take shelter beneath the Tree of the Long Leaves. We place at the top of the Tree of the Long Leaves an Eagle who is able to see afar. If he sees in the distance any evil approaching or any danger threatening he will at once warn the people of the Confederacy.

...

 Skill
Central & Main Idea

The eagle might symbolize foresight in watching out for danger. The preservation of peace seems to be an important idea of this passage.

① Introduction

An Introduction to each text provides historical context for your reading as well as information about the author. You will also learn about the genre of the text and the year in which it was written.

② Notes

Many times, while working through the activities after each text, you will be asked to **annotate** or **make annotations** about what you are reading. This means that you should highlight or underline words in the text and use the "Notes" column to make comments or jot down any questions you have. You may also want to note any unfamiliar vocabulary words here.

You will also see sample student annotations to go along with the Skill lesson for that text.

③ First Read

During your first reading of each selection, you should just try to get a general idea of the content and message of the reading. Don't worry if there are parts you don't understand or words that are unfamiliar to you. You'll have an opportunity later to dive deeper into the text.

④ Think Questions

These questions will ask you to start thinking critically about the text, asking specific questions about its purpose, and making connections to your prior knowledge and reading experiences. To answer these questions, you should go back to the text and draw upon specific evidence to support your responses. You will also begin to explore some of the more challenging vocabulary words in the selection.

⑤ Skills

Each Skill includes two parts: Checklist and Your Turn. In the Checklist, you will learn the process for analyzing the text. The model student annotations in the text provide examples of how you might make your own notes following the instructions in the Checklist. In the Your Turn, you will use those same instructions to practice the skill.

---

③ First Read

Read the Constitution of the Iroquois Nations. After you read, complete the Think Questions below.

④ **THINK QUESTIONS**

1. Do you think that the "Tree of the Great Peace" is real, symbolic, or a combination of both? Support your interpretation with evidence from the text.

2. According to Articles 1 and 10, how did the role of the Onondaga people differ from the roles of the other four tribes of the Iroquois nation? Provide details from the text to support your answer.

3. What does the bundle of arrows in Article 57 symbolize? What does this symbolism suggest is the main purpose of the Iroquois Constitution? Provide details from the text to support your answer.

4. Consider the usage of the word **unanimously** within the text in Article 10. Do you think that the initial letters *un* in *unanimously* refer to the Latin prefix for "one" (as in *unicycle*) or "not" (as in *uncooperative*)? Use evidence from the text to support your answer.

5. Use context to determine the meaning of the word **upbraid** as it is used in the Constitution of the Iroquois Nations. Write your definition of *upbraid* here and explain which context clues helped you determine its meaning.

---

⑤  Skill:
Central or Main Idea

Use the Checklist to analyze Central or Main Idea in the Constitution of the Iroquois Nations. Refer to the sample student annotations about Central or Main Ideas in the text.

⋯ CHECKLIST FOR CENTRAL OR MAIN IDEA

In order to identify two or more central ideas of a text, note the following:

✓ the main idea in each paragraph or group of paragraphs

✓ key details in each paragraph or section of text, distinguishing what they have in common

✓ whether the details contain information that could indicate more than one main idea in a text
  • a science text, for example, may provide information about a specific environment and also a message on ecological awareness
  • a biography may contain equally important ideas about a person's achievements, influence, and the time period in which the person lives or lived

✓ when each central idea emerges

✓ ways that the central ideas interact and build on one another

To determine two or more central ideas of a text and analyze their development over the course of the text, including how they interact and build on one another to provide a complex analysis, consider the following questions:

✓ What main idea(s) do the details in each paragraphs explain or describe?

✓ What central or main ideas do all the paragraphs support?

✓ How do the central ideas interact and build on one another? How does that affect when they emerge?

✓ How might you provide an objective summary of the text? What details would you include?

↻ **YOUR TURN**

1. This question has two parts. First, answer Part A. Then, answer Part B.

   Part A: Which of the following central tenets or beliefs of the Five Nations can be inferred from this passage?

   ○ A. Women had all the political power.
   ○ B. Women decided who could be leaders.
   ○ C. Men had all the political power.
   ○ D. Men decided who could be leaders.

⑤ **Part B:** Which excerpt from the passage best provides evidence to support the answer identified in Part A?

   ○ A. "If a Lord of the Confederacy should seek to establish any authority independent of the jurisdiction of the Confederacy of the Great Peace, which is the Five Nations . . ."
   ○ B. ". . . he shall be warned three times in open council, first by the women relatives . . ."
   ○ C. "If the offending Lord is still obdurate he shall be dismissed by the War Chief . . ."
   ○ D. "His nation shall then install the candidate nominated by the female name holders of his family."

6

NOTES

Skill:
Central or Main
Idea

*This paragraph
discusses the details of
how decisions are made
within the tribes. I
wonder if these details
support a main idea
that the tribes
established procedures
to make decisions even
when there was
disagreement . . . .*

10. In all cases the procedure must be as follows: when the Mohawk and Seneca Lords have **unanimously** agreed upon a question, they shall report their decision to the Cayuga and Oneida Lords who shall deliberate upon the question and report a unanimous decision to the Mohawk Lords. The Mohawk Lords will then report the standing of the case to the Firekeepers, who shall **render** a decision as they see fit in case of a disagreement by the two bodies, or confirm the decisions of the two bodies if they are identical. The Fire Keepers shall then report their decision to the Mohawk Lords who shall announce it to the open council.

11. If through any misunderstanding or obstinacy on the part of the Fire Keepers, they render a decision at variance with that of the Two Sides, the Two Sides shall reconsider the matter and if their decisions are jointly the same as before they shall report to the Fire Keepers who are then compelled to confirm their joint decision.

. . .

Rights, Duties and Qualifications of Lords

. . .

19. If at any time it shall be manifest that a Confederate Lord has not in mind the welfare of the people or disobeys the rules of this Great Law, the men or women of the Confederacy, or both jointly, shall come to the Council and **upbraid** the erring Lord through his War Chief. If the complaint of the people through the War Chief is not heeded the first time it shall be uttered again and then if no attention is given a third complaint and warning shall be given. If the Lord is contumacious the matter shall go to the council of War Chiefs. The War Chiefs shall then divest the erring Lord of his title by order of the women in whom the titleship is vested. When the Lord is deposed the women shall notify the Confederate Lords through their War Chief, and the Confederate Lords shall sanction the act. The women will then select another of their sons as a candidate and the Lords shall elect him. Then shall the chosen one be installed by the Installation Ceremony.

9. When a Lord is to be deposed, his War Chief shall address him as follows:

10. "So you, _____, disregard and set at naught the warnings of your women relatives. So you fling the warnings over your shoulder to cast them behind you.

11. "Behold the brightness of the Sun and in the brightness of the Sun's light I depose you of your title and remove the sacred emblem of your Lordship

---

Close Read

Reread the Constitution of the Iroquois Nations. As you reread, complete the Skills Focus questions below. Then use your answers and annotations from the questions to help you complete the Write activity.

SKILLS FOCUS

1. Explain how the word *binding* relates to one of the main ideas of the Constitution of the Iroquois Nations, citing specific examples from the document to support your response.

2. Identify and summarize important leadership qualities in the Confederacy and explain how the ideas about leadership interact with and build on another main idea in the articles.

3. Explain how sections of the Constitution of the Iroquois Nations remind you of ideas that would eventually shape the early American identity, citing specific evidence from the text to support your response.

WRITE

EXPLANATORY: Most historians believe the Constitution of the Iroquois Nations inspired the framers of the U.S. Constitution. Write a response that explains the similarities between the main ideas of the Constitution of the Iroquois Nations and the principles you believe are relevant in America today. Use evidence from the text and your own experiences to support your response.

6

Close Read & Skills Focus

After you have completed the First Read, you will be asked to go back and read the text more closely and critically. Before you begin your Close Read, you should read through the Skills Focus to get an idea of the concepts you will want to focus on during your second reading. You should work through the Skills Focus by making annotations, highlighting important concepts, and writing notes or questions in the "Notes" column. Depending on instructions from your teacher, you may need to respond online or use a separate piece of paper to start expanding on your thoughts and ideas.

7

Write

Your study of each selection will end with a writing assignment. For this assignment, you should use your notes, annotations, personal ideas, and answers to both the Think and the Skills Focus questions. Be sure to read the prompt carefully and address each part of it in your writing.

Extended Writing Project and Grammar

This is your opportunity to use genre characteristics and craft to compose meaningful, longer written works exploring the theme of each unit. You will draw information from your readings, research, and own life experiences to complete the assignment.

1 Writing Project

After you have read all of the unit text selections, you will move on to a writing project. Each project will guide you through the process of writing your essay. Student models will provide guidance and help you organize your thoughts. One unit ends with an **Extended Oral Project,** which will give you an opportunity to develop your oral language and communication skills.

2 Writing Process Steps

There are four steps in the writing process: Plan, Draft, Revise, and Edit and Publish. During each step, you will form and shape your writing project, and each lesson's peer review will give you the chance to receive feedback from your peers and teacher.

3 Writing Skills

Each Skill lesson focuses on a specific strategy or technique that you will use during your writing project. Each lesson presents a process for applying the skill to your own work and gives you the opportunity to practice it to improve your writing.

Our Lives, Our Fortunes

How do ideologies affect our lives?

> Literary Focus: AMERICAN MODERNISM AND THE HARLEM RENAISSANCE

Texts

 Paired Readings

Copyright © BookheadEd Learning, LLC

Extended Writing Project and Grammar

Talk Back Text   Talk Back Texts are works from a later period that engage with the themes and tropes of the unit's literary focus. Demonstrating that literature is always in conversation, these texts provide dynamic new perspectives to complement the unit's more traditional chronology.

Unit 4: Our Lives, Our Fortunes
How do ideologies affect our lives?

CHIMAMANDA NGOZI ADICHIE

Chimamanda Ngozi Adichie (b. 1977) grew up in Nigeria and studied medicine at the University of Nigeria before leaving for the United States to study communications and political science in Philadelphia at Drexel University. She later completed a master's degree from Johns Hopkins University and received a master of arts in African Studies from Yale University. Her novel *Americanah* (2013) was selected as one of "The 10 Best Books of 2013," and won the National Book Critics Circle Award for Fiction. She was awarded a MacArthur Fellowship in 2008.

JOHN F. CARTER JR.

John Franklin Carter Jr. (1897–1967) grew up in Fall River, Massachusetts, and attended Yale University. A prolific writer, Carter wrote everything from detective novels to presidential speeches. Carter also wrote a twelve-year syndicated column entitled "We, the People," under the pseudonym Jay Franklin, in which he predicted the then-unexpected victory of Harry S Truman in the 1948 presidential election.

KATE CHOPIN

A popular short story writer, Kate Chopin (1850–1904) sparked controversy with the publication of her novel *The Awakening* in 1899. Though it was consistent with much of her previous work that probed the inner lives of strong, independent female characters, the novel scandalized audiences with its frank depiction of female sexuality. Married at age twenty, Chopin moved from St. Louis, Missouri, to Louisiana, where most of her stories are set. She began to write only after being widowed at the age of thirty-one.

PAUL LAURENCE DUNBAR

Born the son of freed slaves from Kentucky, Paul Laurence Dunbar (1872–1906) published his first poem before he graduated from high school. Dunbar briefly worked as an editor for the *Dayton Tattler*, a newspaper published by classmate Orville Wright. Unable to afford law school and rejected by newspapers because of the color of his skin, Dunbar became an elevator operator. He wrote in his spare time, self-published the collection *Oak and Ivy*, published poems and essays in newspapers nationwide, and eventually achieved international acclaim.

ALICE DUNBAR-NELSON

Activist and author Alice Dunbar-Nelson (1875–1936) was born in New Orleans, Louisiana, and began her schoolteacher career after graduating Straight University in 1892. Three years later, she published her first collection of short stories and poems, *Violets and Other Tales*. She later became politically active and helped organize for the women's suffrage movement. In 1918 she worked for the Women's Committee of the Council of Defense, and in 1924 she campaigned for the Dyer Anti-Lynching Bill. She died in Philadelphia at the age of sixty.

RALPH ELLISON

Ralph Waldo Ellison (1914–1994) is best known for his novel *Invisible Man*, which won the National Book Award. He was born in Oklahoma City, Oklahoma, attended the Tuskegee Institute in Alabama, and then moved to New York City. There, he lived at a YMCA on 135th Street in Harlem and met Langston Hughes and Richard Wright. He was not drafted into World War II but did enlist in the United States Merchant Marine. Later, he made money writing book reviews but focused on writing *Invisible Man*. He died of pancreatic cancer at the age of eighty-one.

WILLIAM FAULKNER

Nobel Prize–winning author, screenwriter, and two-time winner of the Pulitzer Prize, William Faulkner (1897–1962) was born in Mississippi. He never graduated from high school, but due to his World War I service, he was able to attend the University of Mississippi. Faulkner published his first novel in 1927 to mixed reviews. His next two novels were poorly received, and his publisher dropped him. Penniless, Faulkner began what would become his fourth novel, *The Sound and the Fury*. His short story "A Rose for Emily" was published the next year.

F. SCOTT FITZGERALD

Author of *This Side of Paradise* and *The Great Gatsby*, F. Scott Fitzgerald (1896–1940) was raised mostly in upstate New York. While attending Princeton University, Fitzgerald was placed on academic probation; he dropped out and joined the army and was commissioned as a second lieutenant just before World War I ended. While stationed at Camp Sheridan in Alabama, he met his future wife, Zelda Sayre, beginning a dramatic courtship that took them from New York City, Paris, and the French Riviera into the salons of the artistic expatriate community.

CHARLOTTE PERKINS GILMAN

After giving birth to her first child, Charlotte Perkins Gilman (1860–1935) documented her depression in her diary. Her doctor prescribed the Rest Cure, which included having her child with her all the time, limiting "intellectual life" to two hours a day, and never writing again. Gilman's anxiety and depression and the prescribed cure inspired her short story "The Yellow Wallpaper." Her depression lifted when she divorced her husband and moved to California. She became involved in the feminist and women's suffrage movements and lectured across the country.

ERNEST HEMINGWAY

During World War I, eighteen-year-old American Ernest Hemingway (1899–1961) was posted to the Italian front as an ambulance driver. After suffering an injury during the war, Hemingway made his way to Paris, where he befriended a group of American expatriate authors and artists. Under their influence, Hemingway developed what have become some of the most celebrated novels and short stories in American fiction. In his 1929 novel *A Farewell to Arms*, Hemingway drew from his wartime experiences as a young man.

LANGSTON HUGHES

When his parents divorced and his father fled to Mexico, Langston Hughes (1902–1967) lived with his grandmother in Lawrence, Kansas, while his mother traveled to find work. Of that time, Hughes noted in his 1940 autobiography *The Big Sea*, "I began to believe in nothing but books and the wonderful world in books—where if people suffered, they suffered in beautiful language, not in monosyllables, as we did in Kansas." Hughes attended Columbia University and sailed around West Africa before becoming a leader of the Harlem Renaissance.

ZORA NEALE HURSTON

When Zora Neale Hurston (1891–1960) was growing up in the all-black town of Eatonville, Florida, she only encountered white people when they passed through the town on their way to or from Orlando. Hurston studied anthropology at Howard, Barnard, and Columbia before dedicating herself to literature. These educational experiences later informed her writing on race and identity. Referencing her time at Barnard, she wrote, "I feel most colored when I am thrown against a sharp white background."

American Modernism

Introduction

This informational text provides readers with cultural and historical information about the time period that gave rise to American Modernism. American Modernism was a literary movement that sought to rebel against the values of the Romantic and Victorian eras. Writers such as Ezra Pound, William Faulkner, Gertrude Stein, and F. Scott Fitzgerald were part of a generation of creative minds that were wearied by the violence and horror of World War I. Their disillusionment led them to experiment with new forms and themes in their work, leading to classics such as *The Great Gatsby* and *As I Lay Dying*. Discover how the volatility of the time period led to innovative writing techniques that came to define American Modernism.

"The Great War had shattered people's perceptions of the world."

1   When you were a small child, you probably thought your parents knew everything and could do anything. When you became a teenager, however, things changed. Suddenly, adults didn't seem so brilliant and amazing. They may have even seemed stubborn and foolish. Even worse is the realization when you become an adult that the certainty you once thought all adults naturally possessed is suddenly nowhere to be found. These rude awakenings capture the feelings of Modernism (1914–1945), a movement of writers and artists who realized that traditional artistic conventions had little to offer when it came to finding meaning in a world suddenly and violently thrust into modernity after global war.

After the Great War

American airforce personnel loading shells into the back of a lorry, circa 1917.

2   On June 28, 1914, a Bosnian Serb named Gavrilo Princip shot and killed Archduke Franz Ferdinand, heir presumptive of the Austrian-Hungarian Empire. There had been tensions and smaller conflicts for years, and the

Please note that excerpts and passages in the StudySync® library and this workbook are intended as touchstones to generate interest in an author's work. The excerpts and passages do not substitute for the reading of entire texts, and StudySync® strongly recommends that students seek out and purchase the whole literary or informational work in order to experience it as the author intended. Links to online resellers are available in our digital library. In addition, complete works may be ordered through an authorized reseller by filling out and returning to StudySync® the order form enclosed in this workbook.

Reading & Writing Companion   1

NOTES

assassination set off a chain of war declarations as nations pledged to support their allies or oppose their enemies. Thus began a war of unprecedented scale: a World War. When America entered the Great War, or, as we now call it, **World War I**, in 1917, they found a new type of warfare. Machine guns, mustard gas, tanks, airplanes, submarines, and other advancements changed the way wars were fought. Young soldiers who grew up hearing tales of glory instead found chaos and brutality. The Great War showed that the world was not as beautiful and polite as the Romantics and Victorians had claimed. Soldiers, women, young people, and others were disillusioned with traditional values, and a growing artistic movement spoke to the desire to rebel against tradition: Modernism.

3   Many works that are considered examples of early Modernism come from Europe, but the movement quickly spread to America thanks in large part to the **Lost Generation**. The term, usually credited to writer Gertrude Stein, often signifies a group of American writers who lived in Europe after the war. This included Stein herself, Ernest Hemingway, F. Scott Fitzgerald, Ezra Pound, T. S. Eliot, and many others.

Ernest Hemingway Returning from Spain

Ernest Hemingway, noted writer, pictured aboard the S.S. Normandie, on arrival in New York City, May 18th. He returned from Spain where he spent ten weeks reporting the war.

4   Many of these **expatriates** flocked to Paris. Here, they wrote and painted and composed. Their work was popular both in Europe and in America. Ironically, some of the most influential works of American literature were being written outside of America.

Breaking Boundaries

5   Modernism did not just break national boundaries. Modernist writers looked for ways to break other conventions. They experimented with different styles and forms, like nontraditional plot lines, fragmented reality, and an absence of third-person omniscient narration. In Europe, Virginia Woolf, James Joyce, and Dorothy Richardson leveraged a technique called stream of consciousness. American author William Faulkner used this technique in his books *The Sound and the Fury* and *As I Lay Dying*. Stream of consciousness is a type of first-person narration. It seeks to mimic the actual flow of our thoughts, which are usually not so organized and grammatically accurate as literature tends to be.

6   Traditionally, earlier literature reflected the common belief that the poor and struggling had done something to deserve their hardships. Modernists challenged this concept of moral order and broke conventions, often by being critical of religion and society and writing about flawed and inadequate protagonists. This is not to say that their writing was always realistic. Modernists rebelled against realism because they believed its themes and settings were too limited.

7   Like all major movements Modernism had smaller sub-movements. **Imagism** is perhaps the best-known sub-movement within Modernist poetry. Prominent Modernist Ezra Pound was a leader of Imagism and promoted the form. In contrast to previous styles of poetry, Imagism offers little guidance to the reader. Instead, an Imagist seeks to present an image and leave the interpretation to the reader. The speaker of the poem is kept unobtrusive and adjectives are used sparingly. Imagist poems are generally in free verse but use a steady rhythm, which helps to distinguish them from regular prose.

8   **Major Concepts**
   - **Irony—**Many people today use *ironic* to say something is coincidental, curious, or even comical. Its actual meaning is "unexpected." A villainous character who becomes the hero of a story, for example, would be ironic. Since so much of Modernism was about subverting literary and social norms, **irony** became a major feature of the movement.

   - **Rejection of Tradition—**Modernism often rejected traditional beliefs and ideas. Character traits, plotlines, and even the conventions of grammar would be used in unconventional ways. Experimental styles and forms were favored. One of the problems in defining Modernism is that, by its nature, it seeks to break rules.

   - **Alienation—**Modernist protagonists often have a strong sense of alienation, or isolation from the world. Since Modernism rejects certain aspects of society, it is natural that the character, in turn, feels out of place

NOTES

in and rejected by society. This feeling of alienation is powerfully exemplified in the character of Jay Gatsby in F. Scott Fitzgerald's *The Great Gatsby.*

9 **Style and Form**

- American Modernist poetry pushed the boundaries of subject matter, form, and style. Poets found inspiration in a wide variety of sources and sought new ways of capturing individual experiences.

- Modernist fiction writers broke from literary tradition. They flouted conventions of grammar, and omitted standard beginnings, transitions, and endings in order to tell stories that reproduced the complex ways in which people think. Ernest Hemingway's short story, "Out of Season," for example, is a Modernist story that has a non-standard beginning and ending.

- Stream of consciousness, which tries to reflect the chaotic flow of thoughts in a person's mind, is a popular Modernist technique.

10 The Great War had shattered people's perceptions of the world. The old powers in Europe had weakened and America was starting to take its place as a world superpower. New technology and ideas had changed the status quo. Modernism was a new movement for a new world. What are examples of popular art or literature that don't follow the typical rules?

Literary Focus

Read "Literary Focus: American Modernism." After you read, complete the Think Questions below.

☁ THINK QUESTIONS

1. What was the significance of World War I for the Modernist movement? Support your response with evidence from the text.

2. How is stream-of-consciousness similar to first-person point of view, and how is it different? Support your response with evidence from the text.

3. What is unusual about Imagism? Support your response with evidence from the text.

4. Use context clues to determine the meaning of the term **Lost Generation**. Write your best definition, along with the words and phrases that were most helpful in determining the meaning of the term. Then, check an encyclopedia to confirm your understanding.

5. The word **expatriate** likely stems from the Latin *ex-*, meaning "away," and *patria*, or "native country." With this information in mind and using context clues from the text, write your best definition of the word *expatriate* as it is used in this text. Cite any words or phrases that were particularly helpful in coming to your conclusion.

Please note that excerpts and passages in the StudySync® library and this workbook are intended as touchstones to generate interest in an author's work. The excerpts and passages do not substitute for the reading of entire texts, and StudySync® strongly recommends that students seek out and purchase the whole literary or informational work in order to experience it as the author intended. Links to online resellers are available in our digital library. In addition, complete works may be ordered through an authorized reseller by filling out and returning to StudySync® the order form enclosed in this workbook.

Reading & Writing Companion 5

The Yellow Wallpaper

FICTION
Charlotte Perkins Gilman
1892

Introduction

Charlotte Perkins Gilman (1860–1935) was an American author and social reformer. She wrote her best-known short story, "The Yellow Wallpaper," after being ordered by her doctor to take a "rest cure" to recover from depression. The result of three months of desperate boredom, this story was sent by Gilman to her doctor as a critique of the sexism in the medical establishment. "The Yellow Wallpaper" follows a sickly wife who has grown bored while on bed rest in the nursery room of a rambling mansion. With a secret journal as her only distraction, she documents an increasing obsession with the wallpaper.

"... these nervous troubles are dreadfully depressing."

Copyright © BookheadEd Learning, LLC

1   It is very seldom that mere ordinary people like John and myself secure ancestral halls for the summer.

2   A colonial mansion, a hereditary estate, I would say a haunted house, and reach the height of romantic felicity—but that would be asking too much of fate!

3   Still I will proudly declare that there is something queer about it.

4   Else, why should it be let so cheaply? And why have stood so long untenanted?

Charlotte Perkins Gilman

5   John laughs at me, of course, but one expects that in marriage.

6   John is practical in the extreme. He has no patience with faith, an **intense** horror of superstition, and he scoffs openly at any talk of things not to be felt and seen and put down in figures.

7   John is a physician, and PERHAPS—(I would not say it to a living soul, of course, but this is dead paper and a great relief to my mind)—PERHAPS that is one reason I do not get well faster.

8   You see he does not believe I am sick!

9   And what can one do?

10 If a physician of high standing, and one's own husband, **assures** friends and relatives that there is really nothing the matter with one but temporary nervous depression—a slight hysterical tendency—what is one to do?

11 My brother is also a physician, and also of high standing, and he says the same thing.

NOTES

12 So I take phosphates or phosphites—whichever it is, and tonics, and journeys, and air, and exercise, and am absolutely forbidden to "work" until I am well again.

13 Personally, I disagree with their ideas.

14 Personally, I believe that congenial work, with excitement and change, would do me good.

15 But what is one to do?

16 I did write for a while in spite of them; but it DOES exhaust me a good deal—having to be so sly about it, or else meet with heavy opposition.

17 I sometimes fancy that in my **condition** if I had less opposition and more society and stimulus—but John says the very worst thing I can do is to think about my condition, and I confess it always makes me feel bad.

18 So I will let it alone and talk about the house.

19 The most beautiful place! It is quite alone, standing well back from the road, quite three miles from the village. It makes me think of English places that you read about, for there are hedges and walls and gates that lock, and lots of separate little houses for the gardeners and people.

20 There is a DELICIOUS garden! I never saw such a garden—large and shady, full of box-bordered paths, and lined with long grape-covered arbors with seats under them.

21 There were greenhouses, too, but they are all broken now.

22 There was some legal trouble, I believe, something about the heirs and coheirs; anyhow, the place has been empty for years.

23 That spoils my ghostliness, I am afraid, but I don't care—there is something strange about the house—I can feel it.

24 I even said so to John one moonlight evening, but he said what I felt was a DRAUGHT, and shut the window.

25 I get unreasonably angry with John sometimes. I'm sure I never used to be so sensitive. I think it is due to this nervous condition.

26 But John says if I feel so, I shall neglect proper self-control; so I take pains to control myself—before him, at least, and that makes me very tired.

27   I don't like our room a bit. I wanted one downstairs that opened on the piazza and had roses all over the window, and such pretty old-fashioned chintz hangings! but John would not hear of it.

28   He said there was only one window and not room for two beds, and no near room for him if he took another.

29   He is very careful and loving, and hardly lets me stir without special direction.

30   I have a schedule prescription for each hour in the day; he takes all care from me, and so I feel basely ungrateful not to value it more.

31   He said we came here solely on my account, that I was to have perfect rest and all the air I could get. "Your exercise depends on your strength, my dear," said he, "and your food somewhat on your appetite; but air you can absorb all the time." So we took the nursery at the top of the house.

32   It is a big, airy room, the whole floor nearly, with windows that look all ways, and air and sunshine galore. It was nursery first and then playroom and gymnasium, I should judge; for the windows are barred for little children, and there are rings and things in the walls.

33   The paint and paper look as if a boys' school had used it. It is stripped off— the paper—in great patches all around the head of my bed, about as far as I can reach, and in a great place on the other side of the room low down. I never saw a worse paper in my life.

34   One of those sprawling flamboyant patterns committing every artistic sin.

35   It is dull enough to confuse the eye in following, pronounced enough to constantly irritate and provoke study, and when you follow the lame uncertain curves for a little distance they suddenly commit suicide—plunge off at outrageous angles, destroy themselves in unheard of contradictions.

36   The color is repellent, almost revolting; a smouldering unclean yellow, strangely faded by the slow-turning sunlight.

37   It is a dull yet lurid orange in some places, a sickly sulphur tint in others.

38   No wonder the children hated it! I should hate it myself if I had to live in this room long. There comes John, and I must put this away,—he hates to have me write a word.

• • •

39 We have been here two weeks, and I haven't felt like writing before, since that first day.

40 I am sitting by the window now, up in this atrocious nursery, and there is nothing to hinder my writing as much as I please, save lack of strength.

41 John is away all day, and even some nights when his cases are serious.

42 I am glad my case is not serious!

43 But these nervous troubles are dreadfully depressing.

44 John does not know how much I really suffer. He knows there is no REASON to suffer, and that satisfies him.

45 Of course it is only nervousness. It does weigh on me so not to do my duty in any way!

46 I meant to be such a help to John, such a real rest and comfort, and here I am a comparative burden already!

47 Nobody would believe what an effort it is to do what little I am able,—to dress and entertain, and order things.

48 It is fortunate Mary is so good with the baby. Such a dear baby!

49 And yet I CANNOT be with him, it makes me so nervous.

Skill: Connotation and Denotation

The use of the word "fancies" seems to have a negative connotation here. The use of this word in the context suggests that the husband is belittling the wife's requests.

50 I suppose John never was nervous in his life. He laughs at me so about this wall-paper!

51 At first he meant to repaper the room, but afterwards he said that I was letting it get the better of me, and that nothing was worse for a nervous patient than to give way to such fancies.

52 He said that after the wall-paper was changed it would be the heavy bedstead, and then the barred windows, and then that gate at the head of the stairs, and so on.

53 "You know the place is doing you good," he said, "and really, dear, I don't care to **renovate** the house just for a three months' rental."

54 "Then do let us go downstairs," I said, "there are such pretty rooms there."

NOTES

55 Then he took me in his arms and called me a blessed little goose, and said he would go down to the cellar, if I wished, and have it whitewashed into the bargain.

56 But he is right enough about the beds and windows and things.

57 It is an airy and comfortable room as any one need wish, and, of course, I would not be so silly as to make him uncomfortable just for a whim.

58 I'm really getting quite fond of the big room, all but that horrid paper.

59 Out of one window I can see the garden, those mysterious deepshaded arbors, the riotous old-fashioned flowers, and bushes and gnarly trees.

60 Out of another I get a lovely view of the bay and a little private wharf belonging to the estate. There is a beautiful shaded lane that runs down there from the house. I always fancy I see people walking in these numerous paths and arbors, but John has cautioned me not to give way to fancy in the least. He says that with my imaginative power and habit of story-making, a nervous weakness like mine is sure to lead to all manner of excited fancies, and that I ought to use my will and good sense to check the tendency. So I try.

61 I think sometimes that if I were only well enough to write a little it would relieve the press of ideas and rest me.

62 But I find I get pretty tired when I try.

63 It is so discouraging not to have any advice and companionship about my work. When I get really well, John says we will ask Cousin Henry and Julia down for a long visit; but he says he would as soon put fireworks in my pillow-case as to let me have those stimulating people about now.

64 I wish I could get well faster.

65 But I must not think about that. This paper looks to me as if it KNEW what a vicious influence it had!

66 There is a recurrent spot where the pattern lolls like a broken neck and two bulbous eyes stare at you upside down.

67 I get positively angry with the impertinence of it and the everlastingness. Up and down and sideways they crawl, and those absurd, unblinking eyes are everywhere. There is one place where two breadths didn't match, and the eyes go all up and down the line, one a little higher than the other.

Please note that excerpts and passages in the StudySync® library and this workbook are intended as touchstones to generate interest in an author's work. The excerpts and passages do not substitute for the reading of entire texts, and StudySync® strongly recommends that students seek out and purchase the whole literary or informational work in order to experience it as the author intended. Links to online resellers are available in our digital library. In addition, complete works may be ordered through an authorized reseller by filling out and returning to StudySync® the order form enclosed in this workbook.

68   I never saw so much expression in an inanimate thing before, and we all know how much expression they have! I used to lie awake as a child and get more entertainment and terror out of blank walls and plain furniture than most children could find in a toy store.

69   I remember what a kindly wink the knobs of our big, old bureau used to have, and there was one chair that always seemed like a strong friend.

70   I used to feel that if any of the other things looked too fierce I could always hop into that chair and be safe.

71   The furniture in this room is no worse than inharmonious, however, for we had to bring it all from downstairs. I suppose when this was used as a playroom they had to take the nursery things out, and no wonder! I never saw such ravages as the children have made here.

72   The wall-paper, as I said before, is torn off in spots, and it sticketh closer than a brother—they must have had perseverance as well as hatred.

73   Then the floor is scratched and gouged and splintered, the plaster itself is dug out here and there, and this great heavy bed which is all we found in the room, looks as if it had been through the wars.

74   But I don't mind it a bit—only the paper.

75   There comes John's sister. Such a dear girl as she is, and so careful of me! I must not let her find me writing.

76   She is a perfect and enthusiastic housekeeper, and hopes for no better profession. I verily believe she thinks it is the writing which made me sick!

77   But I can write when she is out, and see her a long way off from these windows.

78   There is one that commands the road, a lovely shaded winding road, and one that just looks off over the country. A lovely country, too, full of great elms and velvet meadows.

79   This wall-paper has a kind of sub-pattern in a different shade, a particularly irritating one, for you can only see it in certain lights, and not clearly then.

80   But in the places where it isn't faded and where the sun is just so—I can see a strange, provoking, formless sort of figure, that seems to skulk about behind that silly and conspicuous front design.

81   There's sister on the stairs!

• • •

82 Well, the Fourth of July is over! The people are gone and I am tired out. John thought it might do me good to see a little company, so we just had mother and Nellie and the children down for a week.

83 Of course I didn't do a thing. Jennie sees to everything now.

84 But it tired me all the same.

85 John says if I don't pick up faster he shall send me to Weir Mitchell in the fall.

86 But I don't want to go there at all. I had a friend who was in his hands once, and she says he is just like John and my brother, only more so!

87 Besides, it is such an undertaking to go so far.

88 I don't feel as if it was worth while to turn my hand over for anything, and I'm getting dreadfully fretful and querulous.

89 I cry at nothing, and cry most of the time.

90 Of course I don't when John is here, or anybody else, but when I am alone.

91 And I am alone a good deal just now. John is kept in town very often by serious cases, and Jennie is good and lets me alone when I want her to.

92 So I walk a little in the garden or down that lovely lane, sit on the porch under the roses, and lie down up here a good deal.

93 I'm getting really fond of the room in spite of the wall-paper. Perhaps BECAUSE of the wall-paper.

94 It dwells in my mind so!

95 I lie here on this great immovable bed—it is nailed down, I believe—and follow that pattern about by the hour. It is as good as gymnastics, I assure you. I start, we'll say, at the bottom, down in the corner over there where it has not been touched, and I determine for the thousandth time that I WILL follow that pointless pattern to some sort of a conclusion.

96 I know a little of the principle of design, and I know this thing was not arranged on any laws of radiation, or alternation, or repetition, or symmetry, or anything else that I ever heard of.

97 It is repeated, of course, by the breadths, but not otherwise.

98   Looked at in one way each breadth stands alone, the bloated curves and flourishes—a kind of "debased Romanesque" with delirium tremens—go waddling up and down in isolated columns of fatuity.

99   But, on the other hand, they connect diagonally, and the sprawling outlines run off in great slanting waves of optic horror, like a lot of wallowing seaweeds in full chase.

100   The whole thing goes horizontally, too, at least it seems so, and I exhaust myself in trying to **distinguish** the order of its going in that direction.

101   They have used a horizontal breadth for a frieze, and that adds wonderfully to the confusion.

102   There is one end of the room where it is almost intact, and there, when the crosslights fade and the low sun shines directly upon it, I can almost fancy radiation after all,—the interminable grotesques seem to form around a common centre and rush off in headlong plunges of equal distraction.

103   It makes me tired to follow it. I will take a nap I guess.

104   I don't know why I should write this.

105   I don't want to.

106   I don't feel able.

107   And I know John would think it absurd. But I MUST say what I feel and think in some way—it is such a relief!

108   But the effort is getting to be greater than the relief.

109   Half the time now I am awfully lazy, and lie down ever so much.

110   John says I musn't lose my strength, and has me take cod liver oil and lots of tonics and things, to say nothing of ale and wine and rare meat.

111   Dear John! He loves me very dearly, and hates to have me sick. I tried to have a real earnest reasonable talk with him the other day, and tell him how I wish he would let me go and make a visit to Cousin Henry and Julia.

112   But he said I wasn't able to go, nor able to stand it after I got there; and I did not make out a very good case for myself, for I was crying before I had finished.

Copyright © BookheadEd Learning, LLC

113   It is getting to be a great effort for me to think straight. Just this nervous weakness I suppose.

114   And dear John gathered me up in his arms, and just carried me upstairs and laid me on the bed, and sat by me and read to me till it tired my head.

115   He said I was his darling and his comfort and all he had, and that I must take care of myself for his sake, and keep well.

116   He says no one but myself can help me out of it, that I must use my will and self-control and not let any silly fancies run away with me.

117   There's one comfort, the baby is well and happy, and does not have to occupy this nursery with the horrid wall-paper.

118   If we had not used it, that blessed child would have! What a fortunate escape! Why, I wouldn't have a child of mine, an impressionable little thing, live in such a room for worlds.

119   I never thought of it before, but it is lucky that John kept me here after all, I can stand it so much easier than a baby, you see.

120   Of course I never mention it to them any more—I am too wise,—but I keep watch of it all the same.

121   There are things in that paper that nobody knows but me, or ever will.

122   Behind that outside pattern the dim shapes get clearer every day.

123   It is always the same shape, only very numerous.

124   And it is like a woman stooping down and creeping about behind that pattern. I don't like it a bit. I wonder—I begin to think—I wish John would take me away from here!

125   It is so hard to talk with John about my case, because he is so wise, and because he loves me so.

126   But I tried it last night.

127   It was moonlight. The moon shines in all around just as the sun does.

128   I hate to see it sometimes, it creeps so slowly, and always comes in by one window or another.

129   John was asleep and I hated to waken him, so I kept still and watched the moonlight on that undulating wall-paper till I felt creepy.

130   The faint figure behind seemed to shake the pattern, just as if she wanted to get out.

131   I got up softly and went to feel and see if the paper DID move, and when I came back John was awake.

132   "What is it, little girl?" he said. "Don't go walking about like that—you'll get cold."

133   I though it was a good time to talk, so I told him that I really was not gaining here, and that I wished he would take me away.

134   "Why darling!" said he, "our lease will be up in three weeks, and I can't see how to leave before.

135   "The repairs are not done at home, and I cannot possibly leave town just now. Of course if you were in any danger, I could and would, but you really are better, dear, whether you can see it or not. I am a doctor, dear, and I know. You are gaining flesh and color, your appetite is better, I feel really much easier about you."

136   "I don't weigh a bit more," said I, "nor as much; and my appetite may be better in the evening when you are here, but it is worse in the morning when you are away!"

137   "Bless her little heart!" said he with a big hug, "she shall be as sick as she pleases! But now let's improve the shining hours by going to sleep, and talk about it in the morning!"

138   "And you won't go away?" I asked gloomily.

139   "Why, how can I, dear? It is only three weeks more and then we will take a nice little trip of a few days while Jennie is getting the house ready. Really dear you are better!"

140   "Better in body perhaps—" I began, and stopped short, for he sat up straight and looked at me with such a stern, reproachful look that I could not say another word.

141   "My darling," said he, "I beg of you, for my sake and for our child's sake, as well as for your own, that you will never for one instant let that idea enter your mind! There is nothing so dangerous, so fascinating, to a temperament like

yours. It is a false and foolish fancy. Can you not trust me as a physician when I tell you so?"

142 So of course I said no more on that score, and we went to sleep before long. He thought I was asleep first, but I wasn't, and lay there for hours trying to decide whether that front pattern and the back pattern really did move together or separately.

143 On a pattern like this, by daylight, there is a lack of sequence, a defiance of law, that is a constant irritant to a normal mind.

144 The color is hideous enough, and unreliable enough, and infuriating enough, but the pattern is torturing.

145 You think you have mastered it, but just as you get well underway in following, it turns a back-somersault and there you are. It slaps you in the face, knocks you down, and tramples upon you. It is like a bad dream.

146 The outside pattern is a florid arabesque, reminding one of a fungus. If you can imagine a toadstool in joints, an interminable string of toadstools, budding and sprouting in endless convolutions—why, that is something like it.

147 That is, sometimes!

148 There is one marked peculiarity about this paper, a thing nobody seems to notice but myself, and that is that it changes as the light changes.

149 When the sun shoots in through the east window—I always watch for that first long, straight ray—it changes so quickly that I never can quite believe it.

150 That is why I watch it always.

151 By moonlight—the moon shines in all night when there is a moon—I wouldn't know it was the same paper.

152 At night in any kind of light, in twilight, candle light, lamplight, and worst of all by moonlight, it becomes bars! The outside pattern I mean, and the woman behind it is as plain as can be.

153 I didn't realize for a long time what the thing was that showed behind, that dim sub-pattern, but now I am quite sure it is a woman.

154 By daylight she is subdued, quiet. I fancy it is the pattern that keeps her so still. It is so puzzling. It keeps me quiet by the hour.

155   I lie down ever so much now. John says it is good for me, and to sleep all I can.

156   Indeed he started the habit by making me lie down for an hour after each meal.

157   It is a very bad habit I am convinced, for you see I don't sleep.

158   And that cultivates deceit, for I don't tell them I'm awake—O no!

159   The fact is I am getting a little afraid of John.

160   He seems very queer sometimes, and even Jennie has an inexplicable look.

161   It strikes me occasionally, just as a scientific hypothesis,—that perhaps it is the paper!

162   I have watched John when he did not know I was looking, and come into the room suddenly on the most innocent excuses, and I've caught him several times LOOKING AT THE PAPER! And Jennie too. I caught Jennie with her hand on it once.

163   She didn't know I was in the room, and when I asked her in a quiet, a very quiet voice, with the most restrained manner possible, what she was doing with the paper—she turned around as if she had been caught stealing, and looked quite angry—asked me why I should frighten her so!

164   Then she said that the paper stained everything it touched, that she had found yellow smooches on all my clothes and John's, and she wished we would be more careful!

165   Did not that sound innocent? But I know she was studying that pattern, and I am determined that nobody shall find it out but myself!

• • •

166   Life is very much more exciting now than it used to be. You see I have something more to expect, to look forward to, to watch. I really do eat better, and am more quiet than I was.

167   John is so pleased to see me improve! He laughed a little the other day, and said I seemed to be flourishing in spite of my wall-paper.

168   I turned it off with a laugh. I had no intention of telling him it was BECAUSE of the wall-paper—he would make fun of me. He might even want to take me away.

NOTES

169   I don't want to leave now until I have found it out. There is a week more, and I think that will be enough.

• • •

170   I'm feeling ever so much better! I don't sleep much at night, for it is so interesting to watch developments; but I sleep a good deal in the daytime.

171   In the daytime it is tiresome and perplexing.

172   There are always new shoots on the fungus, and new shades of yellow all over it. I cannot keep count of them, though I have tried conscientiously.

173   It is the strangest yellow, that wall-paper! It makes me think of all the yellow things I ever saw—not beautiful ones like buttercups, but old foul, bad yellow things.

174   But there is something else about that paper—the smell! I noticed it the moment we came into the room, but with so much air and sun it was not bad. Now we have had a week of fog and rain, and whether the windows are open or not, the smell is here.

175   It creeps all over the house.

176   I find it hovering in the dining-room, skulking in the parlor, hiding in the hall, lying in wait for me on the stairs.

177   It gets into my hair.

178   Even when I go to ride, if I turn my head suddenly and surprise it—there is that smell!

179   Such a peculiar odor, too! I have spent hours in trying to analyze it, to find what it smelled like.

180   It is not bad—at first, and very gentle, but quite the subtlest, most enduring odor I ever met.

181   In this damp weather it is awful, I wake up in the night and find it hanging over me.

182   It used to disturb me at first. I thought seriously of burning the house—to reach the smell.

183   But now I am used to it. The only thing I can think of that it is like is the COLOR of the paper! A yellow smell.

 Skill: Connotation and Denotation

Words like "hovering" and "hiding" that often have a neutral connotation take on a more negative connotation here when paired with words like "creeps" and "skulking." Together these words create a sense of fear.

184   There is a very funny mark on this wall, low down, near the mopboard. A streak that runs round the room. It goes behind every piece of furniture, except the bed, a long, straight, even SMOOCH, as if it had been rubbed over and over.

185   I wonder how it was done and who did it, and what they did it for. Round and round and round—round and round and round—it makes me dizzy!

. . .

186   I really have discovered something at last.

187   Through watching so much at night, when it changes so, I have finally found out.

188   The front pattern DOES move—and no wonder! The woman behind shakes it!

189   Sometimes I think there are a great many women behind, and sometimes only one, and she crawls around fast, and her crawling shakes it all over.

190   Then in the very bright spots she keeps still, and in the very shady spots she just takes hold of the bars and shakes them hard.

191   And she is all the time trying to climb through. But nobody could climb through that pattern—it strangles so; I think that is why it has so many heads.

192   They get through, and then the pattern strangles them off and turns them upside down, and makes their eyes white!

193   If those heads were covered or taken off it would not be half so bad.

. . .

194   I think that woman gets out in the daytime!

195   And I'll tell you why—privately—I've seen her!

196   I can see her out of every one of my windows!

197   It is the same woman, I know, for she is always creeping, and most women do not creep by daylight.

198   I see her on that long road under the trees, creeping along, and when a carriage comes she hides under the blackberry vines.

199   I don't blame her a bit. It must be very humiliating to be caught creeping by daylight!

200   I always lock the door when I creep by daylight. I can't do it at night, for I know John would suspect something at once.

201   And John is so queer now, that I don't want to irritate him. I wish he would take another room! Besides, I don't want anybody to get that woman out at night but myself.

202   I often wonder if I could see her out of all the windows at once.

203   But, turn as fast as I can, I can only see out of one at one time.

204   And though I always see her, she MAY be able to creep faster than I can turn!

205   I have watched her sometimes away off in the open country, creeping as fast as a cloud shadow in a high wind.

. . .

206   If only that top pattern could be gotten off from the under one! I mean to try it, little by little.

207   I have found out another funny thing, but I shan't tell it this time! It does not do to trust people too much.

208   There are only two more days to get this paper off, and I believe John is beginning to notice. I don't like the look in his eyes.

209   And I heard him ask Jennie a lot of professional questions about me. She had a very good report to give.

210   She said I slept a good deal in the daytime.

211   John knows I don't sleep very well at night, for all I'm so quiet!

212   He asked me all sorts of questions, too, and pretended to be very loving and kind.

213   As if I couldn't see through him!

214   Still, I don't wonder he acts so, sleeping under this paper for three months.

215   It only interests me, but I feel sure John and Jennie are secretly affected by it.

. . .

216   Hurrah! This is the last day, but it is enough. John is to stay in town over night, and won't be out until this evening.

217   Jennie wanted to sleep with me—the sly thing! but I told her I should undoubtedly rest better for a night all alone.

218   That was clever, for really I wasn't alone a bit! As soon as it was moonlight and that poor thing began to crawl and shake the pattern, I got up and ran to help her.

219   I pulled and she shook, I shook and she pulled, and before morning we had peeled off yards of that paper.

220   A strip about as high as my head and half around the room.

221   And then when the sun came and that awful pattern began to laugh at me, I declared I would finish it to-day!

222   We go away to-morrow, and they are moving all my furniture down again to leave things as they were before.

223   Jennie looked at the wall in amazement, but I told her merrily that I did it out of pure spite at the vicious thing.

224   She laughed and said she wouldn't mind doing it herself, but I must not get tired.

225   How she betrayed herself that time!

226   But I am here, and no person touches this paper but me—not ALIVE!

227   She tried to get me out of the room—it was too patent! But I said it was so quiet and empty and clean now that I believed I would lie down again and sleep all I could; and not to wake me even for dinner—I would call when I woke.

228   So now she is gone, and the servants are gone, and the things are gone, and there is nothing left but that great bedstead nailed down, with the canvas mattress we found on it.

229   We shall sleep downstairs to-night, and take the boat home to-morrow.

230   I quite enjoy the room, now it is bare again.

231   How those children did tear about here!

232   This bedstead is fairly gnawed!

233   But I must get to work.

234   I have locked the door and thrown the key down into the front path.

235   I don't want to go out, and I don't want to have anybody come in, till John comes.

236   I want to astonish him.

237   I've got a rope up here that even Jennie did not find. If that woman does get out, and tries to get away, I can tie her!

238   But I forgot I could not reach far without anything to stand on!

239   This bed will NOT move!

240   I tried to lift and push it until I was lame, and then I got so angry I bit off a little piece at one corner—but it hurt my teeth.

241   Then I peeled off all the paper I could reach standing on the floor. It sticks horribly and the pattern just enjoys it! All those strangled heads and bulbous eyes and waddling fungus growths just shriek with derision!

242   I am getting angry enough to do something desperate. To jump out of the window would be admirable exercise, but the bars are too strong even to try.

243   Besides I wouldn't do it. Of course not. I know well enough that a step like that is improper and might be misconstrued.

244   I don't like to LOOK out of the windows even—there are so many of those creeping women, and they creep so fast.

245   I wonder if they all come out of that wall-paper as I did?

246   But I am securely fastened now by my well-hidden rope—you don't get ME out in the road there!

247   I suppose I shall have to get back behind the pattern when it comes night, and that is hard!

248   It is so pleasant to be out in this great room and creep around as I please!

249   I don't want to go outside. I won't, even if Jennie asks me to.

250   For outside you have to creep on the ground, and everything is green instead of yellow.

251   But here I can creep smoothly on the floor, and my shoulder just fits in that long smooch around the wall, so I cannot lose my way.

252   Why there's John at the door!

253   It is no use, young man, you can't open it!

254   How he does call and pound!

255   Now he's crying for an axe.

256   It would be a shame to break down that beautiful door!

257   "John dear!" said I in the gentlest voice, "the key is down by the front steps, under a plantain leaf!"

258   That silenced him for a few moments.

259   Then he said—very quietly indeed, "Open the door, my darling!"

260   "I can't," said I. "The key is down by the front door under a plantain leaf!"

261   And then I said it again, several times, very gently and slowly, and said it so often that he had to go and see, and he got it of course, and came in. He stopped short by the door.

262   "What is the matter?" he cried. "For God's sake, what are you doing!"

263   I kept on creeping just the same, but I looked at him over my shoulder.

264   "I've got out at last," said I, "in spite of you and Jane. And I've pulled off most of the paper, so you can't put me back!"

265   Now why should that man have fainted? But he did, and right across my path by the wall, so that I had to creep over him every time!

First Read

Read "The Yellow Wallpaper." After you read, complete the Think Questions below.

1. What is John's opinion of his wife? Use examples from the text to support your answer.

2. How does the protagonist's mental state change throughout the story? Answer using examples from the text.

3. How do the descriptions of the wallpaper alter as the story goes on? Use examples from the text in your answer.

4. Use context clues to determine the meaning of the word **condition** as it is used in "The Yellow Wallpaper." Write your definition of *condition* here, and explain how you figured it out. Then look up the word in a dictionary and check your definition.

5. Use context clues to determine the meaning of **distinguish**. Then look up the word in a dictionary, and compare your definition with the official definition. Write the definition of *distinguish* here.

Please note that excerpts and passages in the StudySync® library and this workbook are intended as touchstones to generate interest in an author's work. The excerpts and passages do not substitute for the reading of entire texts, and StudySync® strongly recommends that students seek out and purchase the whole literary or informational work in order to experience it as the author intended. Links to online resellers are available in our digital library. In addition, complete works may be ordered through an authorized reseller by filling out and returning to StudySync® the order form enclosed in this workbook.

Reading & Writing Companion   25

Skill:
Connotation and Denotation

Use the Checklist to analyze Connotation and Denotation in "The Yellow Wallpaper." Refer to the sample student annotations about Connotation and Denotation in the text.

••• CHECKLIST FOR CONNOTATION AND DENOTATION

In order to identify the denotative meanings of words, use the following steps:

✓ first, note unfamiliar words and phrases; key words used to describe important characters, events, and ideas; or words that inspire an emotional reaction

✓ next, determine and note the denotative meanings of words by consulting a reference material such as a dictionary, glossary, or thesaurus

✓ finally, analyze nuances in the meanings of words with similar denotations

To better understand the meaning of words and phrases as they are used in a text, including connotative meanings, use the following questions as a guide:

✓ What is the genre or subject of the text? Based on context, what do you think the meaning of the word is intended to be?

✓ Is your inference the same as or different from the dictionary definition?

✓ Does the word create a positive, negative, or neutral emotion?

✓ What synonyms or alternative phrasings help you describe the connotative meaning of the word?

To determine the meaning of words and phrases as they are used in a text, including connotative meanings, use the following questions as a guide:

✓ What is the denotative meaning of the word? Is that denotative meaning correct in context?

✓ What possible positive, neutral, or negative connotations might the word have, depending on context?

✓ What textual details signal a particular connotation for the word?

Copyright © BookheadEd Learning, LLC

Skill:
Connotation and Denotation

Reread paragraphs 59–70 of "The Yellow Wallpaper." Then, using the Checklist on the previous page, answer the multiple-choice questions below.

⟳ YOUR TURN

1. Does the protagonist's description of the gardens in the first sentence provide a positive or negative connotation overall?

   ○ A. Overall, the description has a positive connotation due to words such as *garden*, *arbors*, and *flowers*.

   ○ B. Overall, the description has a positive connotation due to words such as *mysterious*, *riotous*, and *gnarly*.

   ○ C. Overall, the description has a negative connotation due to words such as *garden*, *arbors*, and *flowers*.

   ○ D. Overall, the description has a negative connotation due to words such as *mysterious*, *riotous*, and *gnarly*.

2. Which word does not have a positive connotation as used in this excerpt of the text?

   ○ A. entertainment

   ○ B. wink

   ○ C. impertinence

   ○ D. hop

Please note that excerpts and passages in the StudySync® library and this workbook are intended as touchstones to generate interest in an author's work. The excerpts and passages do not substitute for the reading of entire texts, and StudySync® strongly recommends that students seek out and purchase the whole literary or informational work in order to experience it as the author intended. Links to online resellers are available in our digital library. In addition, complete works may be ordered through an authorized reseller by filling out and returning to StudySync® the order form enclosed in this workbook.

Reading & Writing Companion

27

Close Read

Reread "The Yellow Wallpaper." As you reread, complete the Skills Focus questions below. Then use your answers and annotations from the questions to help you complete the Write activity.

◎ SKILLS FOCUS

1. Identify when the narrator first describes the yellow wallpaper. What connotations do the words she uses have, and how do these words reveal her attitude toward the wallpaper?

2. Themes regarding overcoming societal challenges were common during this literary period. What challenge does the narrator overcome? Find evidence of this at the end of the story.

3. Toward the end of the story, the narrator mentions creeping women. Who might they represent? What connection does she have to them? Identify evidence to support your answer.

4. This story examines an ideological clash in the domestic sphere, and the narrator has a strange relationship with her "home" in this story. How does the narrator's temporary home begin to feel more like a prison? Identify evidence from the text to support your answer.

✏ WRITE

LITERARY ANALYSIS: How does the author use connotation to develop the narrator's identity? Make an argument in which you analyze the author's language and explain how a deliberate choice of words shapes the narrator's understanding of herself. Support your response with evidence from the text.

The Story of an Hour

FICTION
Kate Chopin
1894

Introduction

studysync tv

American author Kate Chopin (1850–1904) wrote feminist literature before the genre was even recognized. Her writing is famous for depicting strong, independent women, liberated to a degree that made many in her time uncomfortable. Considered today to be a widely influential work of proto-feminist literature, "The Story of an Hour"—first published in *Vogue* magazine in 1894—is a quintessential Chopin narrative. In this brief, powerful tale, a wife learns that her husband has died suddenly. But her reaction after digesting the news might not be what you'd expect.

"Free! Body and soul free!"

Kate Chopin

1   Knowing that Mrs. Mallard was afflicted with a heart trouble, great care was taken to break to her as gently as possible the news of her husband's death.

2   It was her sister Josephine who told her, in broken sentences; veiled hints that revealed in half concealing. Her husband's friend Richards was there, too, near her. It was he who had been in the newspaper office when intelligence of the railroad disaster was received, with Brently Mallard's name leading the list of "killed." He had only taken the time to assure himself of its truth by a second telegram, and had hastened to **forestall** any less careful, less tender friend in bearing the sad message.

3   She did not hear the story as many women have heard the same, with a paralyzed inability to accept its significance. She wept at once, with sudden, wild abandonment, in her sister's arms. When the storm of grief had spent itself she went away to her room alone. She would have no one follow her.

Skill:
Story Elements

Words such as "comfortable," "roomy," and "delicious breath" describe the setting in a positive way. This seems to contrast with the terrible news Mrs. Mallard has received and how she must be feeling.

4   There stood, facing the open window, a comfortable, roomy armchair. Into this she sank, pressed down by a physical exhaustion that haunted her body and seemed to reach into her soul.

5   She could see in the open square before her house the tops of trees that were all aquiver with the new spring life. The delicious breath of rain was in the air. In the street below a peddler was crying his wares. The notes of a distant song which some one was singing reached her faintly, and countless sparrows were twittering in the eaves.

6   There were patches of blue sky showing here and there through the clouds that had met and piled one above the other in the west facing her window.

7   She sat with her head thrown back upon the cushion of the chair, quite motionless, except when a sob came up into her throat and shook her, as a child who has cried itself to sleep continues to sob in its dreams.

8   She was young, with a fair, calm face, whose lines bespoke repression and even a certain strength. But now there was a dull stare in her eyes, whose gaze was fixed away off yonder on one of those patches of blue sky. It was not a glance of reflection, but rather indicated a suspension of intelligent thought.

9   There was something coming to her and she was waiting for it, fearfully. What was it? She did not know; it was too subtle and elusive to name. But she felt it, creeping out of the sky, reaching toward her through the sounds, the scents, the color that filled the air.

10 Now her bosom rose and fell **tumultuously**. She was beginning to recognize this thing that was approaching to possess her, and she was striving to beat it back with her will—as powerless as her two white slender hands would have been.

11 When she abandoned herself a little whispered word escaped her slightly parted lips. She said it over and over under the breath: "free, free, free!" The vacant stare and the look of terror that had followed it went from her eyes. They stayed keen and bright. Her pulses beat fast, and the coursing blood warmed and relaxed every inch of her body.

12 She did not stop to ask if it were or were not a monstrous joy that held her. A clear and exalted perception enabled her to dismiss the suggestion as trivial.

13 She knew that she would weep again when she saw the kind, tender hands folded in death; the face that had never looked save with love upon her, fixed and gray and dead. But she saw beyond that bitter moment a long procession of years to come that would belong to her **absolutely**. And she opened and spread her arms out to them in welcome.

14 There would be no one to live for during those coming years; she would live for herself. There would be no powerful will bending hers in that blind persistence with which men and women believe they have a right to impose a private will upon a fellow-creature. A kind intention or a cruel intention made the act seem no less a crime as she looked upon it in that brief moment of illumination.

15 And yet she had loved him—sometimes. Often she had not. What did it matter! What could love, the unsolved mystery, count for in the face of this possession of self-assertion which she suddenly recognized as the strongest impulse of her being!

 Skill:
Textual Evidence

The labor Mrs. Mallard put into her marriage shows on her face, which is lined but strong. She is tired from enduring a lack of freedom. The phrase "But now" signals a transition in her state of mind.

NOTES

16 "Free! Body and soul free!" she kept whispering.

17 Josephine was kneeling before the closed door with her lips to the keyhole, imploring for admission. "Louise, open the door! I beg; open the door—you will make yourself ill. What are you doing, Louise? For heaven's sake open the door."

18 "Go away. I am not making myself ill." No; she was drinking in a very **elixir** of life through that open window.

19 Her fancy[1] was running riot along those days ahead of her. Spring days, and summer days, and all sorts of days that would be her own. She breathed a quick prayer that life might be long. It was only yesterday she had thought with a shudder that life might be long.

20 She arose at length and opened the door to her sister's **importunities**. There was a feverish triumph in her eyes, and she carried herself unwittingly like a goddess of Victory. She clasped her sister's waist, and together they descended the stairs. Richards stood waiting for them at the bottom.

21 Some one was opening the front door with a latchkey. It was Brently Mallard who entered, a little travel-stained, composedly carrying his grip-sack and umbrella. He had been far from the scene of the accident, and did not even know there had been one. He stood amazed at Josephine's piercing cry; at Richards' quick motion to screen him from the view of his wife.

22 But Richards was too late.

23 When the doctors came they said she had died of heart disease—of the joy that kills.

Skill:
Textual Evidence

Louise Mallard locks herself in her room because she is distraught about her husband's death. When she exits her room, the words "triumph" and "Victory" show that she feels like she endured a battle and that she won the fight.

---

1. **fancy** the things she was interested in

First Read

Read "The Story of an Hour." After you read, complete the Think Questions below.

THINK QUESTIONS

1. At the beginning of paragraph 9, Mrs. Mallard senses "something coming to her." What is it? What physical effect does it have on her? Cite evidence from the text to support your response.

2. In paragraphs 5 through 9, how do the details about the natural setting outside of Mrs. Mallard's room relate to her emotional state? Point to specific evidence from the text to support your response.

3. At the end of the story, why do the doctors think that Mrs. Mallard died of "the joy that kills"? Do you think their diagnosis is accurate? Cite evidence from the text to support your answer.

4. Use context clues to determine the meaning of the word **elixir**. Then write your best definition of the word here, along with the clues that helped you find it.

5. Use context clues to determine the meaning of the word **absolutely** as it is used in "The Story of an Hour." Write your best definition of *absolutely* here. Then consult a print or online dictionary to confirm its meaning.

Please note that excerpts and passages in the StudySync® library and this workbook are intended as touchstones to generate interest in an author's work. The excerpts and passages do not substitute for the reading of entire texts, and StudySync® strongly recommends that students seek out and purchase the whole literary or informational work in order to experience it as the author intended. Links to online resellers are available in our digital library. In addition, complete works may be ordered through an authorized reseller by filling out and returning to StudySync® the order form enclosed in this workbook.

Reading & Writing Companion   33

Skill:
Textual Evidence

Use the Checklist to analyze Textual Evidence in "The Story of an Hour." Refer to the sample student annotations about Textual Evidence in the text.

••• CHECKLIST FOR TEXTUAL EVIDENCE

In order to support an analysis by citing evidence that is explicitly stated in the text, do the following:

✓ read the text closely and critically

✓ identify what the text says explicitly

✓ find the most relevant textual evidence that supports your analysis

✓ consider why an author explicitly states specific details and information

✓ cite the specific words, phrases, sentences, or paragraphs from the text that support your analysis

✓ determine where evidence in the text still leaves certain matters uncertain or unresolved

In order to interpret implicit meanings in a text by making inferences, do the following:

✓ combine information directly stated in the text with your own knowledge, experiences, and observations

✓ cite the specific words, phrases, sentences, or paragraphs from the text that led to and support this inference

In order to cite textual evidence to support an analysis of what the text says explicitly as well as inferences drawn from the text, consider the following questions:

✓ Have I read the text closely and critically?

✓ What inferences am I making about the text?

✓ What textual evidence am I using to support these inferences?

✓ Am I quoting the evidence from the text correctly?

✓ Does my textual evidence logically relate to my analysis or the inference I am making?

✓ Does evidence in the text still leave certain matters unanswered or unresolved? In what ways?

Copyright © BookheadEd Learning, LLC

Skill:
Textual Evidence

Reread paragraphs 3–7 from "The Story of an Hour." Then, using the Checklist on the previous page, answer the multiple-choice questions below.

⟳ YOUR TURN

1. According to the text, Mrs. Mallard's initial response to her husband's death is different from that of other women because—

   ○ A. she weeps immediately.
   ○ B. she wants to grieve alone.
   ○ C. she sobs like a child.
   ○ D. she would rather be outside.

2. In paragraph 5, which pair of words best supports the claim that the scene outside the window is a symbol of renewal?

   ○ A. distant, faintly
   ○ B. twittering, crying
   ○ C. tops, aquiver
   ○ D. open, life

Please note that excerpts and passages in the StudySync® library and this workbook are intended as touchstones to generate interest in an author's work. The excerpts and passages do not substitute for the reading of entire texts, and StudySync® strongly recommends that students seek out and purchase the whole literary or informational work in order to experience it as the author intended. Links to online resellers are available in our digital library. In addition, complete works may be ordered through an authorized reseller by filling out and returning to StudySync® the order form enclosed in this workbook.

Reading & Writing Companion   35

Skill:
Story Elements

Use the Checklist to analyze Story Elements in "The Story of an Hour." Refer to the sample student annotations about Story Elements in the text.

••• CHECKLIST FOR STORY ELEMENTS

In order to identify the impact of the author's choices regarding how to develop and relate elements of a story or drama, note the following:

✓ where and when the story takes place, who the main characters are, and the main conflict, or problem, in the plot

✓ the order of the action

✓ how the characters are introduced and developed

✓ the impact that the author's choice of setting has on the characters and their attempt to solve the problem

✓ the point of view the author uses, and how this shapes what readers know about the characters in the story

To analyze the impact of the author's choices regarding how to develop and to relate elements of a story or drama, consider the following questions:

✓ How do the author's choices affect the story elements? The development of the plot?

✓ How does the setting influence the characters?

✓ Which elements of the setting impact the plot, in particular the problem the characters face and must solve?

✓ Are there any flashbacks or other story elements that have an effect on the development of events in the plot? How does the author's choice of utilizing a flashback affect this development?

✓ How does the author introduce and develop characters in the story? Why do you think the author made these choices?

Skill:
Story Elements

Reread paragraphs 17–22 from "The Story of an Hour." Then, using the Checklist on the previous page, answer the multiple-choice questions below.

↻ YOUR TURN

1. How does Mrs. Mallard's character develop over the course of the short story?

    ○ A. Mrs. Mallard begins to recognize that prayer is powerful and that she should begin to pray more so that she can live a long life.

    ○ B. Mrs. Mallard begins to recognize that she is now a free and independent women who has escaped a confined, unhappy life, and this brings her relief, hope, and excitement.

    ○ C. Mrs. Mallard begins to recognize that she is an independent women, and this scares her and makes her feel very sad and alone.

    ○ D. Mrs. Mallard transforms from feeling like an uninteresting, boring women to a goddess who will easily be able to find another husband.

2. How does Mrs. Mallard's character development over the course of the short story impact the story's outcome?

    ○ A. Mrs. Mallard's shift from feeling trapped to feeling free is snatched from her at the very end of the story, causing her death because her newfound joy is taken from her.

    ○ B. Mrs. Mallard shifts from feeling trapped to feeling enraged when she finds out her husband is alive, and her anger causes her death.

    ○ C. Mrs. Mallard's shift from feeling trapped to feeling free is snatched from her at the very end of the story, and it causes her death because she is overjoyed that her husband is alive.

    ○ D. Mrs. Mallard shifts from feeling very sad about her husband's death to feeling comforted and relieved that he is alive.

Close Read

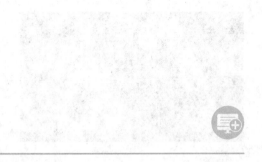

Reread "The Story of an Hour." As you reread, complete the Skills Focus questions below. Then use your answers and annotations from the questions to help you complete the Write activity.

◎ SKILLS FOCUS

1. Identify details in the beginning of the story that describe how other characters perceive Mrs. Mallard, and explain how this characterization helps develop the plot.

2. Paragraphs 4–6 describe aspects of the setting that Mrs. Mallard observes through her window. Highlight the descriptive phrases about the setting that show what Mrs. Mallard sees and explain how these details influence the plot.

3. In paragraphs 9—11, identify textual evidence that shows Mrs. Mallard's reaction to Mr. Mallard's death once she is alone. Then make an inference about how Mrs. Mallard thinks her husband's death will affect her life, and explain how the textual evidence supports that inference.

4. Reread paragraph 14, and use context clues to determine the meaning of the word **impose**. Highlight the clues that help you determine the word's meaning, and annotate with your best definition of the word.

5. What bearing does the ideology of independence have on Mrs. Mallard's feelings and actions? How much does she value independence?

✎ WRITE

LITERARY ANALYSIS: How does the author use story elements such as setting, character development, or theme to develop the plot of "The Story of an Hour"? In your response, evaluate at least two of the story elements used by the author and how they shape the plot. Use evidence from the text to support your analysis.

"These Wild Young People" by One of Them

ARGUMENTATIVE TEXT

John F. Carter Jr.

1920

Introduction

Written in the first year of the Roaring Twenties, this essay by John F. Carter Jr. (1897–1967) examines the stark generational gap that emerged in the years following World War I. The "war to end all wars" left the nations of the world shell-shocked, and one of the young adults of the "wild" generation had a few things to say to those "oldsters" who expected the young to play by the old rules. Carter was well known for his syndicated column, "We, the People," published from 1936 to 1948, during which time he also worked for President Franklin Delano Roosevelt. He went on to write speeches for President Harry S Truman, with whom he had a contentious relationship. In this article published in *The Atlantic*, Carter rebuts the claims made by two critics of the new generation, Katharine Fullerton Gerould and Mr. Grundy.

"We may be fire, but it was they who made us play with gunpowder."

1   For some months past the pages of our more conservative magazines have been crowded with pessimistic descriptions of the younger generation, as seen by their elders and, no doubt, their betters. Hardly a week goes by that I do not read some indignant treatise depicting our extravagance, the corruption of our manners, the futility of our existence, poured out in stiff, scared, shocked sentences before a **sympathetic** and horrified audience of fathers, mothers, and maiden aunts—but particularly maiden aunts.

2   In the May issue of the *Atlantic Monthly* appeared an article entitled "Polite Society," by a certain Mr. Grundy, the husband of a very old friend of my family. In a kindly manner he

*Mentioned our virtues, it is true
But dwelt upon our vices, too.*

"Chivalry and Modesty are dead. Modesty died first," quoth he, but expressed the pious hope that all might yet be well if the oldsters would but be content to "wait and see." His article is one of the best-tempered and most gentlemanly of this long series of Jeremiads[1] against 'these wild young people.' It is significant that it should be anonymous. In reading it, I could not help but be drawn to Mr. Grundy personally, but was forced to the conclusion that he, like everyone else who is writing about my generation, has very little idea of what he is talking about. I would not offend him for the world, and if I apostrophize[2] him somewhat brutally in the following paragraphs, it is only because I am talking of him generically; also because his self-styled 'cousin' is present.

3   For Mrs. Katharine Fullerton Gerould has come forward as the latest volunteer prosecuting attorney, in her powerful 'Reflections of a Grundy Cousin' in the August *Atlantic*. She has little or no patience with us. She disposes of all previous explanations of our degeneration in a series of short paragraphs,

---

1. **Jeremiads** long written works in which someone passionately expresses grief about the state of society; the word is an eponym and refers to the Biblical prophet Jeremiah and the Book of Lamentations
2. **apostrophize** to quote a literary work or song in the middle of a speech or essay

then launches into her own explanation: the decay of religion. She treats it as a primary cause, and with considerable effect. But I think she errs in not attempting to analyze the causes for such decay, which would bring her nearer to the **ultimate** truth.

4 A friend of mine has an uncle who, in his youth, was a wild, fast, extravagant young blood. His clothes were the amazement of even his fastest friends. He drank, he swore, he gambled, bringing his misdeeds to a climax by eloping with an heiress, a beautiful Philadelphian seraph[3], fascinated by this glittering Lucifer. Her family disowned her, and they fled to a distant and wild country. He was, in effect, a brilliant, worthless, attractive, and romantic person. Now he is the sedate deacon of a Boston Presbyterian church, very strong on morality in every shape, a terror to the young, with an impeccable business career, and a very dull family circle. Mrs. Gerould must know of similar cases; so why multiply instances? Just think how moral and unentertaining our generation will be when we have emerged from the 'roaring forties'!—and rejoice.

5 There is a story, illustrative of Californian civic pride, about a California funeral. The friends and relatives of the departed were gathered mournfully around the bier, awaiting the arrival of the preacher who was to deliver the funeral oration. They waited and waited and waited, but no preacher appeared. Finally, a messenger-boy arrived with a telegram. It was from the clergyman, and informed them that he had missed his train. The chief mourner rose to the occasion and asked if anyone would like to say a few kind words about the deceased. No one stirred. Finally a long, lanky person got up, cleared his throat, and drawled, "Wa-a-al, if no one else is goin' to speak, I'd like to say a few things about Los Angeles!"

6 I would like to say a few things about my generation.

7 In the first place, I would like to observe that the older generation had certainly pretty well ruined this world before passing it on to us. They give us this Thing, knocked to pieces, leaky, red-hot, threatening to blow up; and then they are surprised that we don't accept it with the same attitude of pretty, decorous enthusiasm with which they received it, 'way back in the eighteen-nineties, nicely painted, smoothly running, practically foolproof. "So simple that a child can run it!" But the child couldn't steer it. He hit every possible telegraph-pole, some of them twice, and ended with a head-on collision for which *we* shall have to pay the fines and damages. Now, with loving pride, they turn over their wreck to us; and, since we are not properly overwhelmed with loving gratitude, shake their heads and sigh, "Dear! dear! We were so much better-mannered than these wild young people. But then we had the

---

3. **seraph** one who is of the six-winged, highest level of angels in the celestial order

advantages of a good, strict, old-fashioned bringing-up!" How intensely *human* these oldsters are, after all, and how fallible! How they always blame us for not following precisely in their eminently correct footsteps!

8   Then again there is the matter of outlook. When these sentimental old world-wreckers were young, the world was such a different place—at least, so I gather from H.G. Wells's picture of the nineties, in *Joan and Peter*[4]. Life for them was bright and pleasant. Like all normal youngsters, they had their little tin-pot ideals, their sweet little visions, their naive enthusiasms, their nice little sets of beliefs. Christianity had emerged from the blow dealt by Darwin[5], emerged rather in the shape of social dogma. Man was a noble and perfectible creature. Women were angels (whom they smugly sweated in their industries and prostituted in their slums). Right was downing might. The nobility and the divine mission of the race were factors that led our fathers to work wholeheartedly for a millennium, which they caught a glimpse of just around the turn of the century. Why, there were Hague Tribunals[6]! International peace was at last **assured**, and according to current reports, never officially denied, the American delegates held out for the use of poison gas in warfare, just as the men of that generation were later to ruin Wilson's great ideal of a league of nations[7], on the ground that such a scheme was an invasion of American rights. But still, everything, masked by ingrained hypocrisy and prudishness, seemed simple, beautiful, inevitable.

9   Now my generation is disillusionized, and, I think, to a certain extent, brutalized, by the cataclysm which *their* complacent folly engendered. The acceleration of life for us has been so great that into the last few years have been crowded the experiences and the ideas of a normal lifetime. We have in our unregenerate youth learned the practicality and the cynicism that is safe only in unregenerate old age. We have been forced to become realists overnight, instead of idealists, as was our birthright. We have seen man at his lowest, woman at her lightest, in the terrible moral chaos of Europe. We have been forced to question, and in many cases to discard, the religion of our fathers. We have seen hideous peculation, greed, anger, hatred, **malice**, and all uncharitableness, unmasked and rampant and unashamed. We have been forced to live in an atmosphere of "to-morrow we die," and so, naturally, we drank and were merry. We have seen the rottenness and shortcomings of all governments, even the best and most stable. We have seen entire social

---

4. ***Joan and Peter*** a 1918 novel by influential English author H.G. Wells (1866–1946) concerning the situation of English society at the end of World War I
5. **Darwin** Charles Robert Darwin (1809–1882) was a naturalist and author of the 1859 book *On the Origin of Species*, which developed the theory of evolution.
6. **Hague Tribunals** deliberations held at any of the several international courts in Den Haag, Netherlands ("The Hague")
7. **Wilson's great ideal of a league of nations** Initiated by U.S. President Woodrow Wilson (1856–1924), the League of Nations sprang from a peace conference ending World War I as a means for resolving international disputes.

systems overthrown, and our own called in question. In short, we have seen the inherent beastliness of the human race revealed in an infernal apocalypse.

10   It is the older generation who forced us to see all this, which has left us with social and political institutions staggering blind in the fierce white light that, for us, should beat only about the enthroned ideal. And now, through the soft-headed folly of these painfully shocked Grundys, we have that devastating wisdom which is safe only for the burned-out embers of grizzled, cautious old men. We may be fire, but it was they who made us play with gunpowder. And now they are surprised that a great many of us, because they have taken away our apple-cheeked ideals, are seriously considering whether or no *their* game be worth *our* candle.

11   But, in justice to my generation, I think that I must admit that most of us have realized that, whether or no it be worth while, we must all play the game, as long as we are in it. And I think that much of the hectic quality of our life is due to that fact and to that alone. We are faced with staggering problems and are forced to solve them, while the previous incumbents are permitted a graceful and untroubled death. All my friends are working and working hard. Most of the girls I know are working. In one way or another, often unconsciously, the great burden put upon us is being borne, and borne gallantly, by that immodest, unchivalrous set of ne'er-do-wells, so delightfully portrayed by Mr. Grundy and the amazing young Fitzgerald. A keen interest in political and social problems, and

Zelda Sayre and Francis Scott Fitzgerald arm in arm

a determination to face the facts of life, ugly or beautiful, characterizes us, as it certainly did not characterize our fathers. We won't shut our eyes to the truths we have learned. We have faced so many unpleasant things already,—and faced them pretty well,—that it is natural that we should keep it up.

12   Now I think that this is the aspect of our generation that annoys the uncritical and deceives the unsuspecting oldsters who are now met in judgment upon us: our devastating and brutal frankness. And this is the quality in which we really differ from our predecessors. We are frank with each other, frank, or pretty nearly so, with our elders, frank in the way we feel toward life and this badly damaged world. It may be a disquieting and misleading habit, but is it a bad one? We find some few things in the world that we like, and a whole lot that we don't, and we are not afraid to say so or to give our reasons. In earlier generations this was not the case. The young men yearned to be glittering generalities, the young women to act like shy, sweet, innocent fawns toward one another. And now, when grown up, they have come to believe that they

NOTES

actually were figures of pristine excellence, knightly chivalry, adorable modesty, and impeccable propriety. But I really doubt if they were so. Statistics relating to, let us say, the immorality of college students in the eighteen-eighties would not compare favorably with those of the present. However, now, as they look back on it, they see their youth through a mist of muslin, flannels, tennis, bicycles, Tennyson, Browning, and the Blue Danube waltz. The other things, the ugly things that we know about and talk about, must also have been there. But our elders didn't care or didn't dare to consider them, and now they are forgotten. We talk about them unabashed, and not necessarily with Presbyterian disapproval, and so they jump to the conclusion that we are thoroughly bad, and keep pestering us to make us good.

13   The trouble with them is that they can't seem to realize that we are busy, that what pleasure we snatch must be incidental and feverishly hurried. We have to make the most of our time. We actually haven't got so much time for the noble procrastinations of modesty or for the elaborate rigmarole of chivalry, and little patience for the lovely formulas of an ineffective faith. Let them die for a while! They did not seem to serve the world too well in its black hour. If they are inherently good they will come back, vital and untarnished. But just now we have a lot of work, "old time is still a-flying," and we must gather rose-buds while we may.

14   Oh! I know that we are a pretty bad lot, but has not that been true of every **preceding** generation? At least we have the courage to act accordingly. Our music is distinctly barbaric, our girls are distinctly *not* a mixture of arbutus and barbed-wire. We drink when we can and what we can, we gamble, we are extravagant—but we work, and that's about all that we can be expected to do; for, after all, we have just discovered that we are all still very near to the Stone Age. The Grundys shake their heads. They'll *make* us be good. Prohibition is put through to stop our drinking, and hasn't stopped it. Bryan has plans to curtain our philanderings, and he won't do any good. A Draconian[8] code is being hastily formulated at Washington and elsewhere, to prevent us from, by any chance, making any alteration in this present divinely constituted arrangement of things. The oldsters stand dramatically with fingers and toes and noses pressed against the bursting dykes. Let them! They won't do any good. They can shackle us down, and still expect us to repair their blunders, if they wish. But we shall not trouble ourselves very much about them any more. Why should we? What have they done? They have made us work as they never had to work in all their padded lives—but we'll have our cakes and ale for a' that.

---

8. **Draconian** referring to harsh or severe punishment; derived from Draco, legislator of Athens, who instituted strict written codes enforced by law

15 For now we know our way about. We're not babes in the wood, hunting for great, big, red strawberries, and confidently expecting the Robin Redbreasts[9] to cover us up with pretty leaves if we don't find them. We're men and women, long before our time, in the flower of our full-blooded youth. We have brought back into civil life some of the recklessness and ability that we were taught by war. We are also quite fatalistic in our outlook on the tepid perils of tame living. All may yet crash to the ground for aught that we can do about it. Terrible mistakes will be made, but we shall at least make them intelligently and insist, if we are to receive the strictures of the future, on doing pretty much as we choose now.

16 Oh! I suppose that it's too bad that we aren't humble, starry-eyed, shy, respectful innocents, standing reverently at their side for instructions, playing pretty little games, in which they no longer believe, except for us. But we aren't, and the best thing the oldsters can do about it is to go into their respective backyards and dig for worms, great big pink ones—for the Grundy tribe are now just about as important as they are, and they will doubtless make company more congenial and docile than 'these wild young people,' the men and women of my generation.

9. **Robin Redbreasts** a common and traditional nickname for the robin (Erithacus rubecula), a beloved red-breasted bird known for its song and territorial behavior

✏ WRITE

ARGUMENTATIVE: In this argumentative essay, Carter explains that one of the challenges his generation faces is that it is misunderstood and underappreciated. Write an argumentative essay in which you outline the challenges faced by today's youth. What is the greatest challenge facing today's generation? What can be done to help youth address it? Support your argument with evidence from the texts in previous units, outside resources, or your own experiences.

Please note that excerpts and passages in the StudySync® library and this workbook are intended as touchstones to generate interest in an author's work. The excerpts and passages do not substitute for the reading of entire texts, and StudySync® strongly recommends that students seek out and purchase the whole literary or informational work in order to experience it as the author intended. Links to online resellers are available in our digital library. In addition, complete works may be ordered through an authorized reseller by filling out and returning to StudySync® the order form enclosed in this workbook.

Reading & Writing
Companion

45

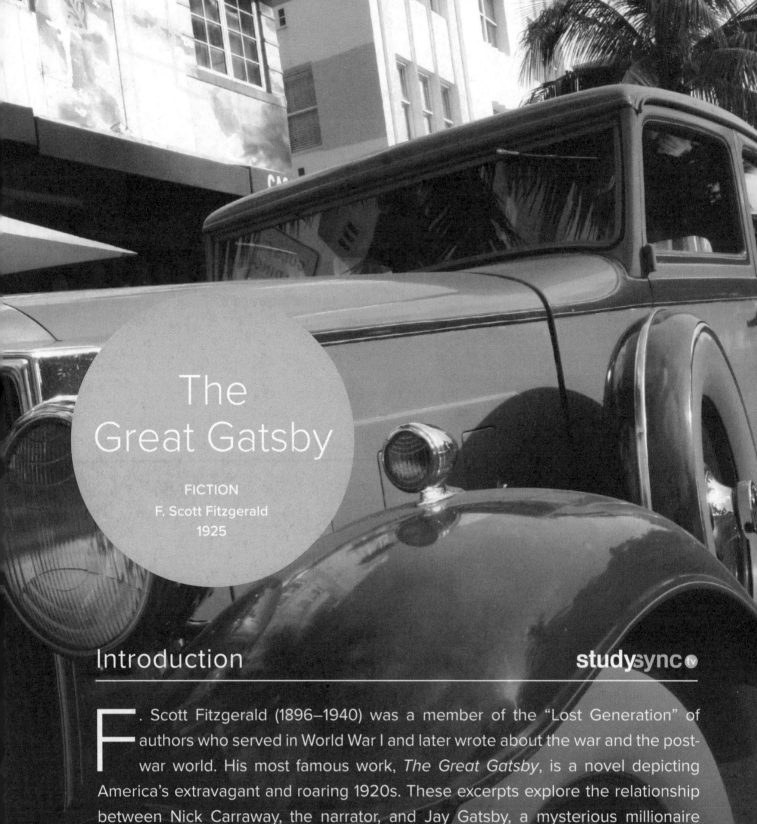

The Great Gatsby

FICTION
F. Scott Fitzgerald
1925

Introduction

studysync tv

F. Scott Fitzgerald (1896–1940) was a member of the "Lost Generation" of authors who served in World War I and later wrote about the war and the post-war world. His most famous work, *The Great Gatsby*, is a novel depicting America's extravagant and roaring 1920s. These excerpts explore the relationship between Nick Carraway, the narrator, and Jay Gatsby, a mysterious millionaire whose lavish parties embody the spirit and spectacle that led Fitzgerald to dub the 1920s "The Jazz Age." As Nick delves into the mystery of Gatsby's past, he finds that the legend of Gatsby is as much a tale of one extraordinary man as it is the story of extraordinary times.

"He smiled understandingly—much more than understandingly."

from Chapter 1

1   In my younger and more vulnerable years my father gave me some advice that I've been turning over in my mind ever since.

2   "Whenever you feel like criticizing any one," he told me, "just remember that all the people in this world haven't had the advantages that you've had."

3   He didn't say any more but we've always been unusually communicative in a reserved way, and I understood that he meant a great deal more than that. In consequence I'm **inclined** to reserve all judgments, a habit that has opened up many curious natures to me and also made me the victim of not a few veteran bores. The abnormal mind is quick to detect and attach itself to this quality when it appears in a normal person, and so it came about that in college I was unjustly accused of being a politician, because I was privy to the secret griefs of wild, unknown men. Most of the confidences were unsought— frequently I have **feigned** sleep, preoccupation, or a hostile levity when I realized by some unmistakable sign that an intimate revelation was quivering on the horizon—for the intimate revelations of young men or at least the terms in which they express them are usually plagiaristic and marred by obvious suppressions. Reserving judgments is a matter of infinite hope. I am still a little afraid of missing something if I forget that, as my father snobbishly suggested, and I snobbishly repeat, a sense of the fundamental decencies is parceled out unequally at birth.

4   And, after boasting this way of my tolerance, I come to the admission that it has a limit. Conduct may be founded on the hard rock or the wet marshes but after a certain point I don't care what it's founded on. When I came back from the East last autumn I felt that I wanted the world to be in uniform and at a sort of moral attention forever; I wanted no more riotous excursions with privileged glimpses into the human heart. Only Gatsby, the man who gives his name to this book, was exempt from my reaction—Gatsby who represented everything for which I have an unaffected scorn. If personality is an unbroken series of successful gestures, then there was something gorgeous about him, some heightened sensitivity to the promises of life, as if he were related to one of

Skill:
Story Elements

Nick is conflicted and has contradictory ideas. This begins to develop his internal moral struggles. He understands his privilege and has values about how people should conduct themselves. A theme of classism begins to emerge.

NOTES

those intricate machines that register earthquakes ten thousand miles away. This responsiveness had nothing to do with that flabby impressionability which is dignified under the name of the "creative temperament"—it was an extraordinary gift for hope, a romantic readiness such as I have never found in any other person and which it is not likely I shall ever find again. No— Gatsby turned out all right at the end; it is what preyed on Gatsby, what foul dust floated in the wake of his dreams that temporarily closed out my interest in the **abortive** sorrows and short-winded elations of men.

. . .

from Chapter 3

5   By midnight the hilarity had increased. A celebrated tenor had sung in Italian, and a notorious contralto had sung in jazz, and between the numbers people were doing "stunts" all over the garden, while happy, vacuous bursts of laughter rose toward the summer sky. A pair of stage twins, who turned out to be the girls in yellow, did a baby act in costume, and champagne was served in glasses bigger than finger-bowls. The moon had risen higher, and floating in the Sound was a triangle of silver scales, trembling a little to the stiff, tinny drip of the banjoes on the lawn.

6   I was still with Jordan Baker. We were sitting at a table with a man of about my age and a rowdy little girl, who gave way upon the slightest provocation to uncontrollable laughter. I was enjoying myself now. I had taken two finger-bowls of champagne, and the scene had changed before my eyes into something significant, elemental, and profound.

7   At a lull in the entertainment the man looked at me and smiled.

8   "Your face is familiar," he said, politely. "Weren't you in the Third Division during the war?"

9   "Why, yes. I was in the ninth machine-gun battalion."

10   "I was in the Seventh Infantry until June nineteen-eighteen. I knew I'd seen you somewhere before."

11   We talked for a moment about some wet, gray little villages in France. Evidently he lived in this vicinity, for he told me that he had just bought a hydroplane, and was going to try it out in the morning.

12   "Want to go with me, old sport? Just near the shore along the Sound."

13   "What time?"

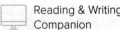

14   "Any time that suits you best."

15   It was on the tip of my tongue to ask his name when Jordan looked around and smiled. "Having a gay time now?" she inquired.

16   "Much better." I turned again to my new acquaintance. "This is an unusual party for me. I haven't even seen the host. I live over there—" I waved my hand at the invisible hedge in the distance, "and this man Gatsby sent over his chauffeur with an invitation." For a moment he looked at me as if he failed to understand.

17   "I'm Gatsby," he said suddenly.

18   "What!" I exclaimed. "Oh, I beg your pardon."

19   "I thought you knew, old sport. I'm afraid I'm not a very good host."

20   He smiled understandingly—much more than understandingly. It was one of those rare smiles with a quality of eternal reassurance in it, that you may come across four or five times in life. It faced—or seemed to face—the whole external world for an instant, and then concentrated on you with an irresistible **prejudice** in your favor. It understood you just so far as you wanted to be understood, believed in you as you would like to believe in yourself, and assured you that it had precisely the impression of you that, at your best, you hoped to convey. Precisely at that point it vanished—and I was looking at an elegant young rough-neck, a year or two over thirty, whose elaborate formality of speech just missed being absurd. Some time before he introduced himself I'd got a strong impression that he was picking his words with care.

21   Almost at the moment when Mr. Gatsby identified himself, a butler hurried toward him with the information that Chicago was calling him on the wire. He excused himself with a small bow that included each of us in turn.

22   "If you want anything just ask for it, old sport," he urged me. "Excuse me. I will rejoin you later." When he was gone I turned immediately to Jordan—constrained to assure her of my surprise. I had expected that Mr. Gatsby would be a florid and corpulent person in his middle years. "Who is he?" I demanded. "Do you know?"

23   "He's just a man named Gatsby."

24   "Where is he from, I mean? And what does he do?"

25 "Now you're started on the subject," she answered with a wan smile. "Well, he told me once he was an Oxford[1] man."

26 A dim background started to take shape behind him, but at her next remark it faded away. "However, I don't believe it."

27 "Why not?"

28 "I don't know," she insisted, "I just don't think he went there."

29 Something in her tone reminded me of the other girl's "I think he killed a man," and had the effect of stimulating my curiosity. I would have accepted without question the information that Gatsby sprang from the swamps of Louisiana or from the lower East Side of New York. That was comprehensible. But young men didn't—at least in my provincial inexperience I believed they didn't—drift coolly out of nowhere and buy a palace on Long Island Sound[2].

30 "Anyhow, he gives large parties," said Jordan, changing the subject with an **urbane** distaste for the concrete. "And I like large parties. They're so intimate. At small parties there isn't any privacy."

Excerpted from *The Great Gatsby* by F. Scott Fitzgerald, published by Scribner.

---

1. **Oxford** the University of Oxford, the oldest university in the English-speaking world, founded in 1096
2. **Long Island Sound** a body of water between Long Island, New York, and the Connecticut shore

First Read

Read *The Great Gatsby.* After you read, complete the Think Questions below.

☁ THINK QUESTIONS

1. What was the advice Nick's father gave him as a youth, and what has been the result of Nick's following this advice? Use details from the text to support your answer.

2. Based on what Nick tells the reader in Chapter 1, what seems to be his attitude toward Gatsby? Provide details from the text that support your response.

3. How did Nick's first impression on meeting Gatsby compare to his prior expectations of the man? Support your answer with textual evidence.

4. Use context and your knowledge of word parts to determine the meaning of the word **feigned** as it is used in paragraph 3. Write your definition of *feign* here and explain the reasoning that led to that definition.

5. Analyze the word **urbane** to provide a possible meaning based on its base word and affix(es). Explain how the context clues in the sentence help you confirm or revise your predicted definition of *urbane,* and explain your process for figuring out its meaning.

Please note that excerpts and passages in the StudySync® library and this workbook are intended as touchstones to generate interest in an author's work. The excerpts and passages do not substitute for the reading of entire texts, and StudySync® strongly recommends that students seek out and purchase the whole literary or informational work in order to experience it as the author intended. Links to online resellers are available in our digital library. In addition, complete works may be ordered through an authorized reseller by filling out and returning to StudySync® the order form enclosed in this workbook.

Reading & Writing Companion

51

Skill:
Story Elements

Use the Checklist to analyze Story Elements in *The Great Gatsby*. Refer to the sample student annotations about Story Elements in the text.

In order to identify the impact of the author's choices regarding how to develop and relate elements of a story or drama, note the following:

✓ where and when the story takes place, who the main characters are, and the main conflict, or problem, in the plot

✓ the order of the action

✓ how the characters are introduced and developed

✓ the impact that the author's choice of setting has on the characters and their attempt to solve the problem

✓ the point of view the author uses, and how this shapes what readers know about the characters in the story

To analyze the impact of the author's choices regarding how to develop and relate elements of a story or drama, consider the following questions:

✓ How do the author's choices affect the story elements? The development of the plot?

✓ How does the setting influence the characters?

✓ Which elements of the setting impact the plot, in particular the problem the characters face and must solve? How does this contribute to the theme?

✓ How does the author's choice of utilizing foreshadowing affect the development of the plot or characters?

  • *Foreshadowing* uses words or phrases that hint at something that is going to happen without revealing the story or spoiling the suspense.

✓ How does the author introduce and develop characters in the story? Why do you think the author made these choices?

Skill:
Story Elements

Reread paragraphs 6–19 of *The Great Gatsby.* Then, using the Checklist on the previous page, answer the multiple-choice questions below.

↻ YOUR TURN

1. What does the text in paragraphs 6 and 15–17 reveal about Nick's character, and how does this contribute to a theme in the story?

   ○ A. Nick feels right at home at Gatsby's party and easily connects with the guests, which influences the theme of materialism.

   ○ B. Nick has insulted Gatsby, which influences the theme of friendship and relationships.

   ○ C. Nick feels guilty attending a party with grand entertainment and finger-bowls of champagne, which influences the theme that pleasure is a sin.

   ○ D. Nick feels some discomfort about the way he was invited to the party, which develops the theme about how conflicting values and standards of conduct reveal class division.

2. How does Nick's first encounter with Gatsby foreshadow the development of Gatsby's intriguing character?

   ○ A. The way in which Gatsby reveals himself to Nick is uncomfortable but also curious, which foreshadows the development of Gatsby's complex, elusive character, as well as Nick's conflicted feelings about him.

   ○ B. The way in which Gatsby reveals himself to Nick is strange and bizarre, which foreshadows the development of Gatsby's disturbed character, as well as Nick's fear of him.

   ○ C. The way in which Gatsby reveals himself to Nick is strange but also cordial, which foreshadows the development of Gatsby's dishonest, disturbed character, as well as Nick's conflicted feelings about him.

   ○ D. The way in which Gatsby reveals himself to Nick is exciting and amusing, which foreshadows the development of Gatsby's outgoing character, as well as Nick's desire to become his good friend.

Please note that excerpts and passages in the StudySync® library and this workbook are intended as touchstones to generate interest in an author's work. The excerpts and passages do not substitute for the reading of entire texts, and StudySync® strongly recommends that students seek out and purchase the whole literary or informational work in order to experience it as the author intended. Links to online resellers are available in our digital library. In addition, complete works may be ordered through an authorized reseller by filling out and returning to StudySync® the order form enclosed in this workbook.

Reading & Writing Companion   53

Close Read

Reread *The Great Gatsby*. As you reread, complete the Skills Focus questions below. Then use your answers and annotations from the questions to help you complete the Write activity.

◎ SKILLS FOCUS

1. What is the significance of the advice that Nick's father gives him? What is ironic about it? Identify evidence from the text to support your answer.

2. Identify an instance when Nick experiences a moral dilemma. Determine how Nick's behavior contributes to the dilemma, and then analyze how this moral dilemma demonstrates a theme.

3. Identify a passage that describes the historical context of the novel. How does the setting reveal details about Gatsby?

4. Identify the passage in which Nick describes his encounter with Gatsby. What is his first impression? Identify evidence from the text to support your answer.

5. What does Nick learn about the danger of equating winning with wealth and class? Identify evidence from the text to support your answer.

✏ WRITE

LITERARY ANALYSIS: In the early twentieth century, American writers turned to Modernism as a form of expression. Through their writing, they shared their disillusioned view of the world after World War I. Drawing on the context you gained in reading "'These Wild Young People,' by One of Them," analyze the thoughts, words, and actions of the characters in *The Great Gatsby* and argue how they reflect elements of this literary period. Support your response with evidence from the text.

A Farewell to Arms

FICTION
Ernest Hemingway
1920

Introduction

Known for a life of adventure, American author Ernest Hemingway (1899–1961) based his semi-autobiographical novel *A Farewell to Arms* on his experiences as an ambulance driver in Italy during World War I. The story revolves around the exploits of Lieutenant ("Tenente") Frederic Henry—also an ambulance driver with the Italian Army—and his doomed romance with a British nurse. In this excerpt, Henry engages the drivers under his command in a philosophical debate about war.

"'Were you there, Tenente, when they wouldn't attack and they shot every tenth man?'"

from Chapter 9

1   "Were you there, Tenente, when they wouldn't attack and they shot every tenth man?"

2   "No."

3   "It is true. They lined them up afterward and took every tenth man. Carabinieri[1] shot them."

4   "Carabinieri," said Passini and spat on the floor. "But those grenadiers[2]; all over six feet. They wouldn't attack."

5   "If everybody would not attack the war would be over," Manera said.

6   "It wasn't that way with the granatieri[3]. They were afraid. The officers all came from such good families."

7   "Some of the officers went alone."

8   "A sergeant shot two officers who would not get out."

9   "Some troops went out."

10   "Those that went out were not lined up when they took the tenth man."

11   "One of those shot by the carabinieri is from my town," Passini said. "He was a big smart tall boy to be in the granatieri. Always in Rome. Always with the girls. Always with the carabinieri." He laughed. "Now they have a guard outside his house with a bayonet and nobody can come to see his mother and father and sisters and his father loses his **civil** rights and cannot even

---

1. **carabinieri** a militarized Italian police force
2. **grenadiers** soldiers who specialize in the use of grenades
3. **granatieri** a mechanized brigade in the Italian armed forces

vote. They are all without law to protect them. Anybody can take their property."

12 "If it wasn't that that happens to their families nobody would go to the attack."

13 "Yes. Alpini would. These V. E. soldiers would. Some bersaglieri[4]."

14 "Bersaglieri have run too. Now they try to forget it."

15 "You should not let us talk this way, Tenente. Evviva l'esercito[5]," Passini said sarcastically.
"I know how you talk," I said. "But as long as you drive the cars and behave—"

16 "—and don't talk so other officers can hear," Manera finished.

17 "I believe we should get the war over," I said. "It would not finish it if one side stopped fighting. It would only be worse if we stopped fighting."

18 "It could not be worse," Passini said respectfully. "There is nothing worse than war."

19 "Defeat is worse."

20 "I do not believe it," Passini said still respectfully. "What is defeat? You go home."

21 "They come after you. They take your home. They take your sisters."

22 "I don't believe it," Passini said. "They can't do that to everybody. Let everybody **defend** his home. Let them keep their sisters in the house."

23 "They hang you. They come and make you be a soldier again. Not in the auto-ambulance, in the **infantry**."

24 "They can't hang every one."

25 "An outside nation can't make you be a soldier," Manera said. "At the first battle you all run."

26 "Like the Tchecos[6]."

---

4. **bersaglieri** members of a light infantry unit in the Italian armed forces
5. **Evviva l'esercito** Italian for "Long live the army"
6. **Tchecos** a person who hails from what is now the Czech Republic

Reading & Writing Companion

27 "I think you do not know anything about being conquered and so you think it is not bad."

28 "Tenente," Passini said. "We understand you let us talk. Listen. There is nothing as bad as war. We in the auto-ambulance cannot realize at all how bad it is. When people realize how bad it is they cannot do anything to stop it because they go crazy. There are some people who never realize. There are people who are afraid of their officers. It is with them the war is made."

29 "I know it is bad but we must finish it."

30 "It doesn't finish. There is no finish to a war."

31 "Yes there is."
Passini shook his head.

32 "War is not won by victory. What if we take San Gabriele[7]? What if we take the Carso[8] and Monfalcone[9] and Trieste[10]? Where are we then? Did you see all the far mountains to-day? Do you think we could take all them too? Only if the Austrians stop fighting. One side must stop fighting. Why don't we stop fighting? If they come down into Italy they will get tired and go away. They have their own country. But no, instead there is a war."

33 "You're an **orator**."

34 "We think. We read. We are not peasants. We are mechanics. But even the peasants know better than to believe in a war. Everybody hates this war."

35 "There is a class that controls a country that is stupid and does not realize anything and never can. That is why we have this war."

36 "Also they make money out of it."

37 "Most of them don't," said Passini. "They are too stupid. They do it for nothing. For stupidity."

38 "We must shut up," said Manera. "We talk too much even for the Tenente."

---

7. **San Gabriele** a mountain of high strategic significance in the Italian military struggle against Austria
8. **the Carso** a vast limestone plateau in southwestern modern-day Slovenia and northeastern Italy
9. **Monfalcone** an Italian city on the Adriatic Sea
10. **Trieste** a province in the small strip of land between Slovenia and the Adriatic Sea

39   "He likes it," said Passini. "We will **convert** him."

40   "But now we will shut up," Manera said.

Excerpted from *A Farewell to Arms* by Ernest Hemingway, published by Scribner.

✏ WRITE

DISCUSSION: Think about how Lieutenant ("Tenente") Frederic Henry's point of view about the war contrasts with the perspective of the other drivers. Discuss these questions: What messages about the ideologies of war do you believe are central to each point of view? What might precipitate a change in Tenente's perspective? Provide examples and evidence from the text to support your ideas. Take notes as answers are suggested, and be prepared to share your group's notes with the rest of the class.

Please note that excerpts and passages in the StudySync® library and this workbook are intended as touchstones to generate interest in an author's work. The excerpts and passages do not substitute for the reading of entire texts, and StudySync® strongly recommends that students seek out and purchase the whole literary or informational work in order to experience it as the author intended. Links to online resellers are available in our digital library. In addition, complete works may be ordered through an authorized reseller by filling out and returning to StudySync® the order form enclosed in this workbook.

Reading & Writing Companion   59

A Rose for Emily

FICTION
William Faulkner
1930

Introduction

Although William Faulkner (1897–1962) spurned fame and said that "the artist is of no importance" compared to the artist's work, he remains one of the most famous and acclaimed prose writers in the history of American literature. A former postmaster who lived most of his life in Oxford, Mississippi, Faulkner often wrote of characters haunted by the past of the fictional Mississippi Yoknapatawpha County—a place not so different from his home region of Lafayette County. Many of Faulkner's most noted works are told from multiple points of view, featuring the reflections, observations, and inner thoughts of a multitude of characters. "A Rose for Emily" was Faulkner's first story published in a national magazine, decades before he won the Pulitzer Prize and the Nobel Prize.

"None of the young men were quite good enough for Miss Emily and such."

> Content Advisory: Please be advised that the following text contains mature themes and racial epithets.

I.

1   When Miss Emily Grierson died, our whole town went to her funeral: the men through a sort of respectful affection for a fallen monument, the women mostly out of curiosity to see the inside of her house, which no one save an old man-servant—a combined gardener and cook—had seen in at least ten years.

2   It was a big, squarish frame house that had once been white, decorated with cupolas and spires and scrolled balconies in the heavily lightsome style of the seventies, set on what had once been our most select street. But garages and cotton gins had **encroached** and obliterated even the august names of that neighborhood; only Miss Emily's house was left, lifting its stubborn and coquettish decay above the cotton wagons and the gasoline pumps—an eyesore among eyesores.

3   And now Miss Emily had gone to join the representatives of those august names where they lay in the cedar-bemused cemetery among the ranked and anonymous graves of Union and Confederate soldiers who fell at the battle of Jefferson.

4   Alive, Miss Emily had been a tradition, a duty, and a care; a sort of hereditary obligation upon the town, dating from that day in 1894 when Colonel Sartoris, the mayor—he who fathered the edict that no Negro woman should appear on the streets without an apron—remitted her taxes, the dispensation dating from the death of her father on into perpetuity. Not that Miss Emily would have accepted charity. Colonel Sartoris invented an involved tale to the effect that Miss Emily's father had loaned money to the town, which the town, as a matter of business, preferred this way of repaying. Only a man of Colonel Sartoris'

Please note that excerpts and passages in the StudySync® library and this workbook are intended as touchstones to generate interest in an author's work. The excerpts and passages do not substitute for the reading of entire texts, and StudySync® strongly recommends that students seek out and purchase the whole literary or informational work in order to experience it as the author intended. Links to online resellers are available in our digital library. In addition, complete works may be ordered through an authorized reseller by filling out and returning to StudySync® the order form enclosed in this workbook.

Reading & Writing Companion   61

generation and thought could have invented it, and only a woman could have believed it.

5   When the next generation, with its more modern ideas, became mayors and aldermen, this arrangement created some little dissatisfaction. On the first of the year they mailed her a tax notice. February came, and there was no reply. They wrote her a formal letter, asking her to call at the sheriff's office at her convenience. A week later the mayor wrote her himself, offering to call or to send his car for her, and received in reply a note on paper of an archaic shape, in a thin, flowing calligraphy in faded ink, to the effect that she no longer went out at all. The tax notice was also enclosed, without comment.

6   They called a special meeting of the Board of Aldermen. A deputation waited upon her, knocked at the door through which no visitor had passed since she ceased giving china-painting lessons eight or ten years earlier. They were admitted by the old Negro into a dim hall from which a stairway mounted into still more shadow. It smelled of dust and disuse—a close, dank smell. The Negro led them into the parlor. It was furnished in heavy, leather-covered furniture. When the Negro opened the blinds of one window, they could see that the leather was cracked; and when they sat down, a faint dust rose sluggishly about their thighs, spinning with slow motes in the single sun-ray. On a tarnished gilt easel before the fireplace stood a crayon portrait of Miss Emily's father.

7   They rose when she entered—a small, fat woman in black, with a thin gold chain descending to her waist and vanishing into her belt, leaning on an ebony cane with a tarnished gold head. Her skeleton was small and spare; perhaps that was why what would have been merely plumpness in another was obesity in her. She looked bloated, like a body long submerged in motionless water, and of that pallid hue. Her eyes, lost in the fatty ridges of her face, looked like two small pieces of coal pressed into a lump of dough as they moved from one face to another while the visitors stated their errand.

8   She did not ask them to sit. She just stood in the door and listened quietly until the spokesman came to a stumbling halt. Then they could hear the invisible watch ticking at the end of the gold chain.

9   Her voice was dry and cold. "I have no taxes in Jefferson. Colonel Sartoris explained it to me. Perhaps one of you can gain access to the city records and satisfy yourselves."

10   "But we have. We are the city authorities, Miss Emily. Didn't you get a notice from the sheriff, signed by him?"

11 "I received a paper, yes," Miss Emily said. "Perhaps he considers himself the sheriff . . . I have no taxes in Jefferson."

12 "But there is nothing on the books to show that, you see. We must go by the—"

13 "See Colonel Sartoris. I have no taxes in Jefferson."

14 "But, Miss Emily—"

15 "See Colonel Sartoris." (Colonel Sartoris had been dead almost ten years.) "I have no taxes in Jefferson. Tobe!" The Negro appeared. "Show these gentlemen out."

II.

16 So she vanquished them, horse and foot, just as she had vanquished their fathers thirty years before about the smell.

17 That was two years after her father's death and a short time after her sweetheart—the one we believed would marry her—had deserted her. After her father's death she went out very little; after her sweetheart went away, people hardly saw her at all. A few of the ladies had the temerity to call, but were not received, and the only sign of life about the place was the Negro man—a young man then—going in and out with a market basket.

18 "Just as if a man—any man—could keep a kitchen properly," the ladies said; so they were not surprised when the smell developed. It was another link between the gross, teeming world and the high and mighty Griersons.

19 A neighbor, a woman, complained to the mayor, Judge Stevens, eighty years old.

20 "But what will you have me do about it, madam?" he said.

21 "Why, send her word to stop it," the woman said. "Isn't there a law? "

22 "I'm sure that won't be necessary," Judge Stevens said. "It's probably just a snake or a rat that n----- of hers killed in the yard. I'll speak to him about it."

23 The next day he received two more complaints, one from a man who came in diffident deprecation. "We really must do something about it, Judge. I'd be the last one in the world to bother Miss Emily, but we've got to do something." That night the Board of Aldermen met—three graybeards and one younger man, a member of the rising generation.

Please note that excerpts and passages in the StudySync® library and this workbook are intended as touchstones to generate interest in an author's work. The excerpts and passages do not substitute for the reading of entire texts, and StudySync® strongly recommends that students seek out and purchase the whole literary or informational work in order to experience it as the author intended. Links to online resellers are available in our digital library. In addition, complete works may be ordered through an authorized reseller by filling out and returning to StudySync® the order form enclosed in this workbook.

Reading & Writing Companion

63

24   "It's simple enough," he said. "Send her word to have her place cleaned up. Give her a certain time to do it in, and if she don't . . . "

25   "Dammit, sir," Judge Stevens said, "will you accuse a lady to her face of smelling bad?"

26   So the next night, after midnight, four men crossed Miss Emily's lawn and slunk about the house like burglars, sniffing along the base of the brickwork and at the cellar openings while one of them performed a regular sowing motion with his hand out of a sack slung from his shoulder. They broke open the cellar door and sprinkled lime there, and in all the outbuildings. As they recrossed the lawn, a window that had been dark was lighted and Miss Emily sat in it, the light behind her, and her upright torso motionless as that of an idol. They crept quietly across the lawn and into the shadow of the locusts that lined the street. After a week or two the smell went away.

27   That was when people had begun to feel really sorry for her. People in our town, remembering how old lady Wyatt, her great-aunt, had gone completely crazy at last, believed that the Griersons held themselves a little too high for what they really were. None of the young men were quite good enough for Miss Emily and such. We had long thought of them as a tableau, Miss Emily a slender figure in white in the background, her father a spraddled silhouette in the foreground, his back to her and clutching a horsewhip, the two of them framed by the back-flung front door. So when she got to be thirty and was still single, we were not pleased exactly, but vindicated; even with insanity in the family she wouldn't have turned down all of her chances if they had really materialized.

28   When her father died, it got about that the house was all that was left to her; and in a way, people were glad. At last they could pity Miss Emily. Being left alone, and a pauper, she had become humanized. Now she too would know the old thrill and the old despair of a penny more or less.

29   The day after his death all the ladies prepared to call at the house and offer condolence and aid, as is our custom. Miss Emily met them at the door, dressed as usual and with no trace of grief on her face. She told them that her father was not dead. She did that for three days, with the ministers calling on her, and the doctors, trying to persuade her to let them dispose of the body. Just as they were about to resort to law and force, she broke down, and they buried her father quickly.

30   We did not say she was crazy then. We believed she had to do that. We remembered all the young men her father had driven away, and we knew that with nothing left, she would have to cling to that which had robbed her, as people will.

III.

31   She was sick for a long time. When we saw her again, her hair was cut short, making her look like a girl, with a vague resemblance to those angels in colored church windows—sort of tragic and serene.

32   The town had just let the contracts for paving the sidewalks, and in the summer after her father's death they began the work. The construction company came with n------ and mules and machinery, and a foreman named Homer Barron, a Yankee—a big, dark, ready man, with a big voice and eyes lighter than his face. The little boys would follow in groups to hear him cuss the n------, and the n------ singing in time to the rise and fall of picks. Pretty soon he knew everybody in town. Whenever you heard a lot of laughing anywhere about the square, Homer Barron would be in the center of the group. Presently we began to see him and Miss Emily on Sunday afternoons driving in the yellow-wheeled buggy and the matched team of bays from the livery stable.

33   At first we were glad that Miss Emily would have an interest, because the ladies all said, "Of course a Grierson would not think seriously of a Northerner, a day laborer." But there were still others, older people, who said that even grief could not cause a real lady to forget *noblesse oblige*[1]—without calling it *noblesse oblige*. They just said, "Poor Emily. Her kinsfolk should come to her." She had some kin in Alabama; but years ago her father had fallen out with them over the estate of old lady Wyatt, the crazy woman, and there was no communication between the two families. They had not even been represented at the funeral.

34   And as soon as the old people said, "Poor Emily," the whispering began. "Do you suppose it's really so?" they said to one another. "Of course it is. What else could . . ." This behind their hands; rustling of craned silk and satin behind jalousies closed upon the sun of Sunday afternoon as the thin, swift clop-clop-clop of the matched team passed: "Poor Emily."

35   She carried her head high enough—even when we believed that she was fallen. It was as if she demanded more than ever the recognition of her dignity as the last Grierson; as if it had wanted that touch of earthiness to reaffirm her imperviousness. Like when she bought the rat poison, the arsenic. That was over a year after they had begun to say "Poor Emily," and while the two female cousins were visiting her.

---

1. **noblesse oblige** the implied responsibility of the privileged or wealthy to act with kindness and benevolence

NOTES

36   "I want some poison," she said to the druggist. She was over thirty then, still a slight woman, though thinner than usual, with cold, haughty black eyes in a face the flesh of which was strained across the temples and about the eyesockets as you imagine a lighthouse-keeper's face ought to look. "I want some poison," she said.

37   "Yes, Miss Emily. What kind? For rats and such? I'd recom—"

38   "I want the best you have. I don't care what kind."

39   The druggist named several. "They'll kill anything up to an elephant. But what you want is—"

40   "Arsenic," Miss Emily said. "Is that a good one?"

41   "Is . . . arsenic? Yes, ma'am. But what you want—"

42   "I want arsenic."

43   The druggist looked down at her. She looked back at him, erect, her face like a strained flag. "Why, of course," the druggist said. "If that's what you want. But the law requires you to tell what you are going to use it for."

44   Miss Emily just stared at him, her head tilted back in order to look him eye for eye, until he looked away and went and got the arsenic and wrapped it up. The Negro delivery boy brought her the package; the druggist didn't come back. When she opened the package at home there was written on the box, under the skull and bones: "For rats."

IV.

45   So the next day we all said, "She will kill herself"; and we said it would be the best thing. When she had first begun to be seen with Homer Barron, we had said, "She will marry him." Then we said, "She will persuade him yet," because Homer himself had remarked—he liked men, and it was known that he drank with the younger men in the Elks' Club—that he was not a marrying man. Later we said, "Poor Emily" behind the jalousies as they passed on Sunday afternoon in the glittering buggy, Miss Emily with her head high and Homer Barron with his hat cocked and a cigar in his teeth, reins and whip in a yellow glove.

46   Then some of the ladies began to say that it was a disgrace to the town and a bad example to the young people. The men did not want to interfere, but at last the ladies forced the Baptist minister—Miss Emily's people were Episcopal—to call upon her. He would never divulge what happened during

NOTES

that interview, but he refused to go back again. The next Sunday they again drove about the streets, and the following day the minister's wife wrote to Miss Emily's relations in Alabama.

47 So she had blood-kin under her roof again and we sat back to watch **developments**. At first nothing happened. Then we were sure that they were to be married. We learned that Miss Emily had been to the jeweler's and ordered a man's toilet set in silver, with the letters H. B. on each piece. Two days later we learned that she had bought a complete outfit of men's clothing, including a nightshirt, and we said, "They are married." We were really glad. We were glad because the two female cousins were even more Grierson than Miss Emily had ever been.

48 So we were not surprised when Homer Barron—the streets had been finished some time since—was gone. We were a little disappointed that there was not a public blowing-off, but we believed that he had gone on to prepare for Miss Emily's coming, or to give her a chance to get rid of the cousins. (By that time it was a cabal, and we were all Miss Emily's allies to help circumvent the cousins.) Sure enough, after another week they departed. And, as we had expected all along, within three days Homer Barron was back in town. A neighbor saw the Negro man admit him at the kitchen door at dusk one evening.

49 And that was the last we saw of Homer Barron. And of Miss Emily for some time. The Negro man went in and out with the market basket, but the front door remained closed. Now and then we would see her at a window for a moment, as the men did that night when they sprinkled the lime, but for almost six months she did not appear on the streets. Then we knew that this was to be expected too; as if that quality of her father which had thwarted her woman's life so many times had been too virulent and too furious to die.

50 When we next saw Miss Emily, she had grown fat and her hair was turning gray. During the next few years it grew grayer and grayer until it attained an even pepper-and-salt iron-gray, when it ceased turning. Up to the day of her death at seventy-four it was still that **vigorous** iron-gray, like the hair of an active man.

51 From that time on her front door remained closed, save for a period of six or seven years, when she was about forty, during which she gave lessons in china-painting. She fitted up a studio in one of the downstairs rooms, where the daughters and granddaughters of Colonel Sartoris' contemporaries were sent to her with the same regularity and in the same spirit that they were sent to church on Sundays with a twenty-five-cent piece for the collection plate. Meanwhile her taxes had been remitted.

NOTES

52   Then the newer generation became the backbone and the spirit of the town, and the painting pupils grew up and fell away and did not send their children to her with boxes of color and tedious brushes and pictures cut from the ladies' magazines. The front door closed upon the last one and remained closed for good. When the town got free postal delivery, Miss Emily alone refused to let them fasten the metal numbers above her door and attach a mailbox to it. She would not listen to them.

53   Daily, monthly, yearly we watched the Negro grow grayer and more stooped, going in and out with the market basket. Each December we sent her a tax notice, which would be returned by the post office a week later, unclaimed. Now and then we would see her in one of the downstairs windows—she had evidently shut up the top floor of the house—like the carven torso of an idol in a niche, looking or not looking at us, we could never tell which. Thus she passed from generation to generation—dear, inescapable, **impervious**, tranquil, and perverse.

54   And so she died. Fell ill in the house filled with dust and shadows, with only a doddering Negro man to wait on her. We did not even know she was sick; we had long since given up trying to get any information from the Negro. He talked to no one, probably not even to her, for his voice had grown harsh and rusty, as if from disuse.

55   She died in one of the downstairs rooms, in a heavy walnut bed with a curtain, her gray head propped on a pillow yellow and moldy with age and lack of sunlight.

       V.

56   The Negro met the first of the ladies at the front door and let them in, with their hushed, sibilant voices and their quick, curious glances, and then he disappeared. He walked right through the house and out the back and was not seen again.

57   The two female cousins came at once. They held the funeral on the second day, with the town coming to look at Miss Emily beneath a mass of bought flowers, with the crayon face of her father musing profoundly above the bier and the ladies sibilant and macabre; and the very old men—some in their brushed Confederate uniforms—on the porch and the lawn, talking of Miss Emily as if she had been a contemporary of theirs, believing that they had danced with her and courted her perhaps, confusing time with its mathematical progression, as the old do, to whom all the past is not a **diminishing** road but, instead, a huge meadow which no winter ever quite touches, divided from them now by the narrow bottle-neck of the most recent decade of years.

58   Already we knew that there was one room in that region above stairs which no one had seen in forty years, and which would have to be forced. They waited until Miss Emily was decently in the ground before they opened it.

59   The violence of breaking down the door seemed to fill this room with pervading dust. A thin, acrid pall as of the tomb seemed to lie everywhere upon this room decked and furnished as for a bridal: upon the valance curtains of faded rose color, upon the rose-shaded lights, upon the dressing table, upon the delicate array of crystal and the man's toilet things backed with tarnished silver, silver so tarnished that the monogram was obscured. Among them lay a collar and tie, as if they had just been removed, which, lifted, left upon the surface a pale crescent in the dust. Upon a chair hung the suit, carefully folded; beneath it the two mute shoes and the discarded socks.

60   The man himself lay in the bed.

61   For a long while we just stood there, looking down at the profound and fleshless grin. The body had apparently once lain in the attitude of an embrace, but now the long sleep that outlasts love, that conquers even the grimace of love, had cuckolded him. What was left of him, rotted beneath what was left of the nightshirt, had become inextricable from the bed in which he lay; and upon him and upon the pillow beside him lay that even coating of the patient and biding dust.

62   Then we noticed that in the second pillow was the indentation of a head. One of us lifted something from it, and leaning forward, that faint and invisible dust dry and acrid in the nostrils, we saw a long strand of iron-gray hair.

"A Rose for Emily". Copyright 1930 & renewed 1958 by William Faulkner, from COLLECTED STORIES OF WILLIAM FAULKNER by William Faulkner. Used by permission of W.W. Norton & Company, Inc.

✎ WRITE

NARRATIVE: William Faulkner's stories are often told from multiple points of view. "A Rose for Emily" is told from the point of view of unnamed narrators who harbor their own attitudes towards Emily. In a narrative response, rewrite any section of the story from a different point of view: either that of Emily, her father, Tobe, or a character of your own imagination. Be sure to incorporate and modify specific descriptions and dialogue from the text as needed in your alteration of Faulkner's classic story.

Please note that excerpts and passages in the StudySync® library and this workbook are intended as touchstones to generate interest in an author's work. The excerpts and passages do not substitute for the reading of entire texts, and StudySync® strongly recommends that students seek out and purchase the whole literary or informational work in order to experience it as the author intended. Links to online resellers are available in our digital library. In addition, complete works may be ordered through an authorized reseller by filling out and returning to StudySync® the order form enclosed in this workbook.

Reading & Writing Companion   69

The Harlem Renaissance

Introduction

This informational text offers background information about the historical and cultural circumstances that led to the Harlem Renaissance. After the turn of the 20th century, populations were becoming increasingly urban. African Americans living in Northern cities faced widespread discriminatory practices by city landlords, and those living in the South dealt with the racism and injustice of Jim Crow laws. This oppression, along with the North's newfound need for factory workers, led to both the Great Migration and a migration within New York City to the welcoming Harlem area. Partially a response to racist stereotyping and partially to the horror of the first World War, the Harlem Renaissance was an African American-led artistic movement that came to define the 1920s and early '30s and inspired generations of creative minds to come.

"How do artists of the Harlem Renaissance continue to inspire music and culture today?"

NOTES

1   The Harlem Renaissance was a cultural movement among African Americans in New York City in the 1920s and 1930s. Musicians, writers, and other African American artists were drawn to the Harlem section of Manhattan by plentiful housing. The artistic outpouring lasted until the Great Depression, which forced many Harlem artists to move elsewhere to look for work. The impact of the Harlem Renaissance, however, can still be felt heavily in our culture today.

The Emergence of an African American Community

2   African Americans in New York City began moving to the Harlem area in about 1900. They were eager to move out of the West Side of Manhattan because of the overcrowded apartment buildings and increasing hostility from white neighbors. Harlem had a surplus of apartments, so landlords were eager to welcome African American tenants. When African-American churches began to relocate to Harlem as well, the population of African Americans became solidly established and continued to grow.

3   **Segregation** was widespread in the North as well as the South in the early 1900s. African Americans were banned from many white-owned businesses, including restaurants and hotels. As a result, African Americans started their own businesses to draw on the large number of potential customers in their neighborhood. Among the most successful businesses were nightclubs that featured jazz and blues.

The Great Migration

4   *The Great Migration* is a term that refers to the movement of African Americans from the South to large cities in the North between approximately 1916 and 1940 in its first wave. World War I cut off the flow of European immigrants to the United States. Northern factories were growing and needed more workers. They recruited African Americans from the South to help make up for the shortage of workers. African Americans were eager to leave the South because of Jim Crow laws that led to mistreatment and violence against them. Many were sharecroppers who had difficulty surviving economically, especially when an insect **infestation** decimated the cotton crop during the war. Harlem also attracted black immigrants from the Caribbean, promising greater prosperity and economic opportunity. These movements of people

to large cities were part of a larger trend; in 1920, for the first time in U.S. history, more people lived in urban areas than in rural areas.

An unidentified woman, dressed in a fur-trimmed coat, posing in front of a tree on a Harlem sidewalk, 1920s

A Flowering of the Arts

5   In 1917, playwright Ridgely Torrence's *Three Plays for a Negro Theatre*, often considered among the first major works of the Harlem Renaissance, premiered. The suite of plays featured African-American actors and represented complex characters. The work rejected racial **stereotypes** frequently portrayed in the theater previously. For example, one of the most popular forms of musical entertainment in the late 1800s had been minstrel shows. These shows, featuring white men wearing makeup that made them appear to be African American, consisted of comedy and musical numbers that portrayed African Americans as foolish and simpleminded. In the early 1900s, African American musical performers sought to create their own musical theater that gave a more accurate portrayal of African American life and moved away from stereotypes. Eubie Blake and Noble Sissle wrote a musical called *Shuffle Along* in 1921. It became the first hit Broadway musical written by African Americans.

6   What's more, music attracted people from all races and walks of life to Harlem's nightclubs. This music included the blues, which originated in the Deep South in the late 1800s. The blues grew out of African American spirituals and work songs as well as the music of Africa and folk music. Blues music featured trancelike rhythm and unusual scales and chords.

7   Another musical form, jazz, drew partly from the blues. It, too, was invented by African Americans in the South in the late 1800s. Jazz features **improvisation**, in which the musicians create music as they play rather than reading it from sheets of paper. Bandleaders such as Duke Ellington and performers such as Louis Armstrong created some of the greatest jazz of any era. Jazz was created by African Americans in New Orleans in the late 1800s and represented an integral part of African American culture. It became so popular in the 1920s that the decade is sometimes referred to as the Jazz Age.

8   At the **outset** of the Harlem Renaissance, as African American musicians flocked to Harlem for work in the popular nightclubs, other artists soon followed. African-American artists living in Harlem had the opportunity to be trained and mentored by famous artists and to attend top schools in other parts of New York City. Among the artists who took advantage of these opportunities were painter Aaron Douglas and sculptor Augusta Savage.

9   Rising literacy levels among African Americans in the late 1800s made it possible for African Americans to consider writing as an occupation. Prior to the Civil War, few Southern African Americans could read because it was illegal to give instruction to enslaved persons. The growth of schools in the South for African Americans after the war meant that, when the Great Migration occurred, there was a burgeoning demand for literature and news by and about African Americans. The creation of African-American newspapers and magazines helped meet this need.

10 Among the most important magazines read by people in Harlem were *The Crisis* and *Opportunity: A Journal of Negro Life*. *The Crisis* was published by the National Association for the Advancement of Colored People (NAACP), an organization founded in New York City in 1909. The editor of *The Crisis* was W.E.B. Du Bois, who used the magazine to shed light on the oppression of African Americans and call for increased civil rights. Du Bois, a sociologist, was the leading activist for African Americans during the early 1900s. He appointed Jessie Fauset as literary editor of *The Crisis*. She published works by most of Harlem's leading authors. Another important group of African-American activists, the National Urban League, published *Opportunity*. This journal published, in addition to literature, studies of the difficulties faced by African Americans, including discrimination.

Political Activism Voices of Change

11 At the **outset** of the Harlem Renaissance, Marcus Garvey launched one of the largest mass movements in African American history. Garvey, who had emigrated from Jamaica in 1916, led the Universal Negro Improvement Association. A charismatic speaker, Garvey urged African Americans to become economically strong and suggested that they help form a black-led nation in Africa. He published a newspaper called *Negro World* that ran stories describing achievements of African Americans as well as features about African culture. At its peak his movement had over one million followers. While his ideas could be divisive among members of the Harlem Renaissance movement, his work influenced contemporary political thinking.

12 One of the most widely talented figures in the Harlem Renaissance was James Weldon Johnson. After serving as a **diplomat** to South American countries under President Theodore Roosevelt, Johnson became the first African American to serve as executive secretary of the NAACP. He had

NOTES

distinguished himself within the organization for his campaign against lynching. As leader of the NAACP, he helped to expand the organization and fight limitations on voting rights in the South. Johnson was also talented in poetry and music. He served as a mentor to young poets and collected their work in important anthologies. He and his brother wrote the song "Lift Every Voice and Sing," sometimes referred to today as the Black National Anthem.

Writer and educator James Weldon Johnson (1871–1938) was one of the founders of the NAACP and served as the group's secretary from 1916 to 1930.

13 **Major Concepts**
- **End Stereotypes**—At the time of the Harlem Renaissance, many white people regarded African Americans as not being deserving of equal rights. Negative portrayals of African Americans extended beyond just minstrel shows and could also be found in fiction and motion pictures created by whites. African-American authors worked to **dispel** these images in two ways. First, they portrayed the diversity of African Americans, describing lives in many types of settings. Second, the quality of the literary output of these writers provided strong evidence that they were fully deserving of equal education and equal rights.

- **Protest Oppression**—Harlem writers worked to create a historical record of the injustices endured by African Americans. Lynchings, race riots, and other mob violence were epidemic throughout the period of the Harlem Renaissance. Harlem writers also drew attention to segregation and denials of constitutional rights. Discrimination in all its forms was another important topic.

- **Experiment with Modernism**—The mass slaughter of World War I led many artists to question the traditional beliefs of society. Writers in both Europe and the United States made a break with traditional literary forms and began to experiment. Individuals felt free to explore their own identities and imaginations. Modernist tropes were employed by many Harlem Renaissance writers, such as Jean Toomer's famous engagement with the movement in his novel *Cane* (1923).

NOTES

- **Preserve Heritage**—Many writers who had migrated from the South wrote important works about their experiences there. They wrote about both the positive aspects of African American communities and the negative experiences of persecution by whites. Another important aspect of preserving heritage was writing about Africa. For example, Countee Cullen explored African themes in some of his finest poetry.

- **Everyday Themes**—As part of the effort to combat stereotypes, African American writers in Harlem sought to define and celebrate the common activities of African Americans. An important novel about working-class African Americans was Zora Neale Hurston's *Their Eyes Were Watching God,* which includes elements of magical realism. Poets of the Harlem Renaissance often wrote about challenges common among many African Americans. Claude McKay's "If We Must Die" is a powerful indictment of white violence against African Americans. In Arna Bontemps's "A Black Man Talks of Reaping," the speaker's memories of the anxiety of farming lead to thoughts about the difficulties faced by the next generation.

Style and Form

14 **Influence of Blues and Jazz**

- Jazz and blues strongly influenced the writing style of authors of fiction and poetry during the Harlem Renaissance. It was evident in such literary techniques as rhythm and stream of consciousness, which sometimes mirrored improvised music in style. Such techniques lent a strong Modernist feel to compositions.

- Langston Hughes, one of the leading poets of the twentieth century, spoke about the influence of music on his work. "To me, jazz is a montage of a dream deferred. A great big dream—yet to come—and always *yet*—to become ultimately and finally true." The influence of blues is also evident in Hughes's work. His poem "The Weary Blues" concerns a blues singer and begins,

> Droning a drowsy syncopated tune,
> Rocking back and forth to a mellow croon

15 **Blending the Traditional with the Modern**

- Although Harlem Renaissance writers experimented with Modernist forms, there was a strong traditional streak in their work as well. Zora Neale Hurston collected folklore and oral histories from African Americans in the South while she was a college student. Then she moved to Harlem and drew on this research to create satires and other literary forms. Poets, including Countee Cullen and Claude McKay, used traditional forms such as sonnets to frame their Modernist themes.

- Alain Locke, a professor of philosophy at Howard University, urged Harlem artists to draw on African history and subjects in their work. Locke collected

Please note that excerpts and passages in the StudySync® library and this workbook are intended as touchstones to generate interest in an author's work. The excerpts and passages do not substitute for the reading of entire texts, and StudySync® strongly recommends that students seek out and purchase the whole literary or informational work in order to experience it as the author intended. Links to online resellers are available in our digital library. In addition, complete works may be ordered through an authorized reseller by filling out and returning to StudySync® the order form enclosed in this workbook.

Reading & Writing Companion   75

the work of top Harlem writers in *The New Negro.* This anthology showed the diversity of the African-American experience, which was another way of combating the stereotypes that had grown up around portrayals of African Americans in prior decades.

16   The Great Depression is often considered the moment of the Harlem Renaissance's decline, as many African Americans left Harlem in search of jobs elsewhere. The rich artistic output of Harlem's artists would endure, however. Today, a line can be drawn connecting Harlem Renaissance writers and musicians to poets of the Black Arts Movement in the 1960s, such as Amiri Baraka and Nikki Giovanni, and to hip hop artists, like Kendrick Lamar. The Harlem Renaissance was an artistic movement that brought the social, political, and cultural realities of urban African-American life to mainstream culture and remains widely influential today. How do artists of the Harlem Renaissance continue to inspire music and culture today?

Literary Focus

Read "Literary Focus: The Harlem Renaissance." After you read, complete the Think Questions below.

 THINK QUESTIONS

1. What caused the Great Migration of African Americans from the South to large Northern cities? Cite textual evidence to support your answer.

2. How did the NAACP play an important role in the Harlem Renaissance?

3. How did Harlem Renaissance writers make a break with the traditions of American literature from previous eras? Support your answer with evidence from the text.

4. The word *stereotype* comes from the Greek *stereos*, meaning "solid" and the Latin *typus,* meaning "image." With this information in mind and using context clues, write your best definition of the word **stereotype** as it used in this text. Cite any words or phrases that were particularly helpful in coming to your conclusion.

5. Use context clues to determine the meaning of the word **improvisation**. Write your best definition here, along with the words and phrases that were most helpful in determining the word's meaning. Then, check a dictionary to confirm your understanding.

Alain Locke and the Harlem Renaissance

Introduction

In 1916, African Americans began leaving the American South in record numbers, in what would become known as the Great Migration. Most people settled in urban areas, including Harlem, a neighborhood in New York City. In the 1920s, there was an artistic, social, and intellectual movement based in Harlem called the Harlem Renaissance. The Harlem Renaissance was encouraged and chronicled by Alain Locke, whose anthology, *The New Negro: An Interpretation*, showcased talented African American artists and writers. This anthology discussed African American identity, artistic expression, and self determination.

"... Alain Locke who aspired to both capture and catalyze the significance of Harlem's artists."

NOTES

1   By the turn of the twentieth century, a movement was building. A large contingent of African Americans moved out of the South and into growing communities in the North in conjunction with the Great Migration. Encouraged by job opportunities and seeking a more welcoming place to live, many African Americans came to New York. Over time, an African American community **centered** in the neighborhood of Harlem. The neighborhood swiftly became a vibrant and popular cultural center, the birthplace of a cultural movement known as the Harlem Renaissance.

2   Who was the self-described "midwife" of that movement? He was an academic named Alain Locke who aspired to both capture and catalyze the significance of Harlem's artists.

The New Negro[1] Movement

3   What is now called the "Harlem Renaissance" was referred to at the time as the "Negro Renaissance" or the "New Negro Movement." The "New Negro" was a way contemporary writers, critics, social activists, and intellectuals used to define an African American population less concerned with the artistic

Portrait of Alain Locke by artist Betsy Graves Reyneau.

1. **Negro:** common terminology used at the time to refer to an African American person.

Please note that excerpts and passages in the StudySync® library and this workbook are intended as touchstones to generate interest in an author's work. The excerpts and passages do not substitute for the reading of entire texts, and StudySync® strongly recommends that students seek out and purchase the whole literary or informational work in order to experience it as the author intended. Links to online resellers are available in our digital library. In addition, complete works may be ordered through an authorized reseller by filling out and returning to StudySync® the order form enclosed in this workbook.

Reading & Writing Companion   79

standards of white and European culture, and more interested in self-expression and a distinctive African American culture.

4 It was the concept of the "New Negro," that Howard University philosopher and professor Alain Locke sought to capture through the creation of an anthology. Alain Locke compiled his anthology, *The New Negro: An Interpretation*, in 1925. It contained artistic and sociological texts from a variety of culturally relevant poets, writers, and researchers, such as Langston Hughes, Zora Neale Hurston, Jean Toomer, Claude McKay, and Countee Cullen. Locke included the art and intellectual ideas of African Americans to document the possibilities and achievements of the African American community and to dispel stereotypes, which he believed art, as opposed to direct political activism, was most equipped to do.

5 He hoped to encourage the movement in its efforts to display the identity and achievements of African Americans and, ultimately, to encourage racial pride. In his anthology, Locke acknowledged the work of W.E.B Du Bois. Locke contended that Du Bois' efforts to create and encourage African American art was for propagandistic purposes, to improve the station of African Americans by educating and motivating an audience to accept racial equality. Locke believed he had distinctly different goals for his anthology, concerned that "propaganda perpetuates the position of group inferiority." Locke and other artists believed that art created by African Americans should be allowed to pursue the goals of art, whether that was for the purpose of individual or group expression.

6 Locke solicited pieces for his anthology that resonated with the themes of self-definition and self-expression of African Americans. Within the anthology, there were different expressions of what that meant. Some artists favored distinguishing themselves entirely from white culture, while others emulated the styles of white artists to gain acceptance or to demonstrate their ability to create art that was equally powerful. One of the successes of the collection is how well it represents some of the important and thoroughly debated ideas of the day.

Style and Self-Definition

7 One tension visible in Locke's anthology is the varied approaches towards writing in dialect. "Dialect poetry" was a popular genre at the time, sometimes written in response or opposition to white plantation tradition literature. Some African American poets, such as Paul Dunbar, wrote poems in dialect, like "The Old Cabin," which often departed a great deal in **tone** and content from the dialect poetry of the plantation tradition. However, with the transition into the 1920's, some authors wanted to move away from the focus on slave narratives and the impact of slavery, including styles like dialect poetry that some artists felt did more to perpetuate stereotypes than celebrate folk culture. Jean Toomer's poems in the collection avoid dialect altogether and

Copyright © BookheadEd Learning, LLC

borrow from European styles of poetry, while Zora Neale Hurston's contribution, a short story titled "Spunk," uses dialect to tell the story of an all-African American cast of characters, and plays with the theme of courage. This debate about the use of dialect in writing, which writer Sterling Brown criticized as "an affectation to please a white audience" represented a desire on the part of some African American artists to define their own cultural aesthetic.

The Importance of Heritage

8   Another method of self-expression and racial pride seen in the anthology was an interest in "cultural pluralism," which encouraged an interest in African roots while developing a **unique** African American culture. Locke, in particular, encouraged African Americans to reclaim their African identity and, therefore, a cultural heritage. He was interested in African influences on Caribbean nations and on African Americans and encouraged younger artists to study African culture. In his anthology, he included an essay by W. E. B. Du Bois on the relationship between the "New Negro" movement and events in Africa, including colonialism and struggles for freedom that he believes paralleled the African American plight. Locke chose not to mention Marcus Garvey or his movement, which encouraged African Americans to move to Africa, considering him too controversial a figure and not representative of the "New Negro" he desired to promote.

9   Artists of the time were exploring the idea of an African heritage. Langston Hughes' "The Negro Speaks of Rivers" released prior to the anthology painted the picture of an African-built society, and Africans as a proud and powerful people. Countee Cullen's poem, "Heritage," printed in *The New Negro*, has a more complicated relationship with the concept of African heritage. In it, he repeatedly asks, "What is Africa to me?," highlighting the difficulties of feeling attachment to an African homeland and the culture he has never seen.

Bronze from the Benin kingdom housed in the Ethnological museum in Berlin, Germany. *The New Negro* included an image of a Benin bronze in its pages.

NOTES

10   Part of defining the "New Negro" was in embracing an African aesthetic and in placing value on African American features and skin color, as can be seen in the images of sculptures included in the pages of *The New Negro*. Striking illustrations, also, by Winold Reiss celebrated a variety of skin colors and facial features using realistic artistic techniques to depict the authors represented in the anthology in a way that had not been popularized visually before.

The Writers and the Audience

11   Although *The New Negro* presented a range of diverse **perspectives** on questions at the heart of African American arts and culture, it was not wholly inclusive of African American perspectives. Some contemporary critics, including a writer named Eric Reader, objected to the makeup of the authors in anthology, citing a lack of poor and working-class African Americans. These perspectives, Reader noted, reflected the majority of African Americans.

12   The writers who made up the collection in *The New Negro*, however, were aware that they were writing for a diverse audience. Alain Locke encouraged the African American artists of this generation to turn their awareness and voice inwards to the black community, rather than trying to prove something to a white audience. Langston Hughes echoed this sentiment in his 1926 essay "The Negro Artist and the Racial Mountain," writing, "We young Negro artists who create now intend to express our individual dark-skinned selves without fear or shame. If white people are pleased, we are glad. If they are not, it doesn't matter."

13   The anthology was popular with a white audience at a time when white audiences were increasingly receptive to African American writing. However, an element of the anthology's success across a white audience can be attributed to the allure and "exoticization" of the African American community and Harlem at the time. Still, the writers included in *The New Negro* became more widely published and better paid.

The Anthology Today

14   One of the most beautiful parts of the Harlem Renaissance was the **complexity** of ideas circulating regarding art, race, and African American identity. Members of the Harlem Renaissance were eager that their art and philosophies were not oversimplified: James Weldon Johnson wrote in his book about the period, *Black Manhattan*, that "Harlem is still in the process of making. It is still new and mixed; so mixed that one may get many different views—which is all right so long as one view is not taken to be the whole picture." Locke's anthology captures some of those many perspectives, allowing modern-day readers to understand that the Harlem Renaissance was a multi-faceted movement encompassing many viewpoints.

Literary Seminar: Alain Locke and the Harlem Renaissance

Read "Literary Seminar: Alain Locke and the Harlem Renaissance." After you read, complete the Think Questions below.

☁ THINK QUESTIONS

1. What criticism did *The New Negro* face in regards to the writers chosen for its publication? Cite specific evidence from the text in your response.

2. What were some challenges that Locke and others faced when creating *The New Negro*? Cite relevant evidence from the text in your response.

3. Why didn't Locke include ideas or writing from political leader and writer Marcus Garvey? Identify and select evidence from the text in your answer.

4. Use context clues to determine the meaning of the word **complexity** as it is used in the text. Write your definition of *complexity* here, along with those words from the text that helped you determine its meaning. Then check a dictionary to confirm your understanding.

5. What is the meaning of the word **tone** as it is used in the text? Write your best definition here, along with a brief explanation of how you arrived at its meaning.

Please note that excerpts and passages in the StudySync® library and this workbook are intended as touchstones to generate interest in an author's work. The excerpts and passages do not substitute for the reading of entire texts, and StudySync® strongly recommends that students seek out and purchase the whole literary or informational work in order to experience it as the author intended. Links to online resellers are available in our digital library. In addition, complete works may be ordered through an authorized reseller by filling out and returning to StudySync® the order form enclosed in this workbook.

Reading & Writing Companion   **83**

In Our Neighborhood

FICTION
Alice Dunbar-Nelson
1895

Introduction

Alice Dunbar-Nelson (1875–1935) was born in New Orleans to mixed-race parents. Moving easily between genres, she was a journalist, poet, essayist, diarist, and short story writer. As a woman with African American, Caucasian, Native American, and Creole heritage, she wrote elegantly about the complexities of issues such as racism, family, community, gender, ethnicity, and sexuality. "In Our Neighborhood," from Dunbar-Nelson's first book of stories, *Violets and Other Tales,* is a good example of her sure feel for the ironic nuances of a Southern neighborhood.

"The Harts were going to give a party."

1   The Harts were going to give a party. Neither Mrs. Hart, nor the Misses Hart, nor the small and busy Harts who amused themselves and the neighborhood by continually falling in the gutter on special occasions, had mentioned this fact to anyone, but all the interested denizens of that particular square could tell by the unusual air of bustle and activity which pervaded the Hart **domicile**. Lillian, the æsthetic[1], who furnished theme for many spirited discussions, leaned airily out of the window; her auburn (red) tresses carefully done in curl papers. Martha, the practical, flourished the broom and duster with unwonted activity, which the small boys of the neighborhood, peering through the green shutters of the front door, duly reported to their mammas, busily engaged in holding down their respective door-steps by patiently sitting thereon.

2   Pretty soon, the junior Harts,—two in number—began to travel to and fro, soliciting the loan of a "few chairs," "some nice dishes," and such like things, indispensable to every decent, self-respecting party. But to all inquiries as to the use to which these articles were to be put, they only vouchsafed one reply, "Ma told us as we wasn't to tell, just ask for the things, that's all."

3   Mrs. Tuckley the dress-maker, brought her sewing out on the front-steps, and entered a vigorous protest to her next-door neighbor.

4   "Humph," she sniffed, "mighty funny they can't say what's up. Must be something in it. Couldn't get none o' *my* things, and not invite *me*!"

5   "Did she ask you for any?" absent-mindedly inquired Mrs. Luke, shielding her eyes from the sun.

6   "No-o—, but she'd better sense, she knows *me*—she ain't—mercy me, Stella! Just look at that child tumbling in the mud! You, Stella, come here, I say! Look at you now, there—and there—and there?"

7   The luckless Stella having been soundly cuffed, and sent whimpering in the back-yard, Mrs. Tuckley continued, "Yes as I was saying, 'course, taint none o'

1. **æsthetic**   dated spelling of aesthetic; concerned with beauty or appearance

my business, but I always did wonder how them Harts do keep up. Why, them girls dress just as fine as any lady on the Avenue and that there Lillian wears real diamond ear-rings. 'Pears mighty, mighty funny to me, and Lord the airs they do put on! Holdin' up their heads like nobody's good enough to speak to. I don't like to talk about people, you know, yourself, Mrs. Luke I never speak about anybody, but mark my word, girls that cut up capers like them Hartses' girls never come to any good."

8   Mrs. Luke heaved a deep sigh of appreciation at the wisdom of her neighbor, but before she could reply a re-inforcement in the person of little Mrs. Peters, apron over her head, hands shrivelled and soap-sudsy from washing, appeared.

9   "Did you ever see the like?" she asked in her usual, rapid breathless way. "Why, my Louis says they're putting canvass cloths on the floor, and taking down the bed in the back-room; and putting greenery and such like trash about. Some style about them, eh?"

10 Mrs. Tuckley tossed her head and sniffed contemptuously, Mrs. Luke began to rehearse a time worn tale, how once a carriage had driven up to the Hart house at nine o'clock at night, and a distinguished looking man alighted, went in, stayed about ten minutes and finally drove off with a great clatter. Heads that had shaken ominously over this story before began to shake again, and tongues that had wagged themselves tired with conjectures started now with some brand new ideas and theories. The children of the square, tired of fishing for minnows in the ditches, and making mud-pies in the street, clustered about their mother's skirts receiving occasional slaps, when their attempts at taking part in the conversation became too pronounced.

11 Meanwhile, in the Hart household, all was bustle and preparation. To and fro the members of the house flitted, arranging chairs, putting little touches here and there, washing saucers and glasses, chasing the Hart Juniors about, losing things and calling frantically for each other's assistance to find them. Mama Hart, big, plump and perspiring, puffed here and there like a large, rosy engine, giving impossible orders, and receiving sharp answers to foolish questions. Lillian, the æsthetic, practiced her most graceful poses before the large mirror in the parlor; Martha rushed about, changing the order of the furniture, and Papa Hart, just come in from work, paced the rooms disconsolately, asking for dinner.

12 "Dinner!" screamed Mama Hart, "Dinner, who's got time to fool with dinner this evening? Look in the sideboard and you'll see some bread and ham; eat that and shut up."

NOTES

13 Eight o'clock finally arrived, and with it, the music and some straggling guests. When the first faint chee-chee of the violin floated out into the murky atmosphere, the smaller portion of the neighborhood went straightway into ecstasies. Boys and girls in all stages of deshabille clustered about the door-steps and gave vent to audible exclamations of approval or disapprobation concerning the state of affairs behind the green shutters. It was a warm night and the big round moon sailed serenely in a cloudless, blue sky. Mrs. Tuckley had put on a clean calico wrapper, and planted herself with the indomitable Stella on her steps, "to watch the purceedings."

14 The party was a grand success. Even the **intensely** critical small fry dancing on the pavement without to the scraping and fiddling of the string band, had to admit that. So far as they were concerned it was all right, but what shall we say of the guests within? They who glided easily over the canvassed floors, bowed, and scraped and simpered, "just like the big folks on the Avenue," who ate the ice-cream and cake, and drank the sweet, weak Catawba wine amid boisterous healths to Mr. and Mrs. Hart and the Misses Hart; who smirked and perspired and cracked ancient jokes and heart-rending puns during the intervals of the dances, who shall say that they did not enjoy themselves as thoroughly and as fully as those who frequented the wealthier entertainments up-town.

15 Lillian and Martha in gossamer gowns of pink and blue flitted to and fro attending to the wants of their guests. Mrs. Hart, gorgeous in a black satin affair, all folds and lace and drapery, made desperate efforts to appear cool and collected—and failed miserably. Papa Hart spent one half his time standing in front of the mantle, spreading out his coat-tails, and **benignly** smiling upon the young people, while the other half was devoted to initiating the male portion of the guests into the mysteries of "snake killing."

16 Everybody had said that he or she had had a splendid time, and finally, when the last kisses had been kissed, the last good-byes been said, the whole Hart family sat down in the now deserted and disordered rooms, and sighed with relief that the great event was over at last.

17 "Nice crowd, eh?" remarked Papa Hart. He was brimful of joy and second-class whiskey, so no one paid any attention to him.

18 "But did you see how shamefully Maude flirted with Willie Howard?" said Lillian. Martha tossed her head in disdain; Mr. Howard she had always considered her especial property, so Lillian's observation had a rather disturbing effect.

19   "I'm so warm and tired," cried Mama Hart, plaintively, "children how are we going to sleep to-night?"

20   Thereupon the whole family arose to devise ways and means for wooing the drowsy god. As for the Hart Juniors they had long since solved the problem by falling asleep with sticky hands and faces upon a pile of bed-clothing behind the kitchen door.

21   It was late in the next day before the house had begun to resume anything like its former appearance. The little Harts were kept busy all morning returning chairs and dishes, and distributing the remnants of the feast to the vicinity. The ice-cream had melted into a warm custard, and the cakes had a rather worse for wear appearance, but they were appreciated as much as though just from the confectioner. No one was forgotten, even Mrs. Tuckley, busily stitching on a muslin garment on the steps, and unctuously rolling the latest morsel of scandal under her tongue, was obliged to confess that "them Hartses wasn't such bad people after all, just a bit queer at times."

22   About two o'clock, just as Lillian was re-draping the tidies on the stiff, common plush chairs in the parlor, some one pulled the bell violently. The visitor, a rather good-looking young fellow, with a worried **expression** smiled somewhat sarcastically as he heard a sound of scuffling and running within the house.

23   Presently Mrs. Hart opened the door wiping her hand, red and smoking with dish-water, upon her apron. The worried expression deepened on the visitor's face as he addressed the woman with visible embarrassment.

24   "Er—I—I—suppose you are Mrs. Hart?" he inquired awkwardly.

25   "That's my name, sir," replied she with pretentious dignity.

26   "Er—your-er—may I come in madam?"

27   "Certainly," and she opened the door to admit him, and offered a chair.

28   "Your husband is an employee in the Fisher Oil Mills, is he not?"

29   Mrs. Hart straightened herself with pride as she replied in the affirmative. She had always been proud of Mr. Hart's position as foreman of the big oil mills, and was never so happy as when he was expounding to someone in her presence, the difficulties and intricacies of machine-work.

30 "Well you see my dear Mrs. Hart," continued the visitor. "Now pray don't get excited—there has been an accident, and your husband—has—er—been hurt, you know."

31 But for a painful whitening in her usually rosy face, and a quick compression of her lips, the wife made no sign.

32 "What was the accident?" she queried, leaning her elbows on her knees.

33 "Well, you see, I don't understand machinery and the like, but there was something about a wheel out of gear, and a band bursted, or something, anyhow a big wheel flew to pieces, and as he was standing near, he was hit."

34 "Where?"

35 "Well—well, I may as well tell you the truth, madam; a large piece of the wheel struck him on the head—and—he was killed instantly."

36 She did not faint, nor make any outcry, nor tear her hair as he had partly expected, but sat still staring at him, with a sort of helpless, dumb horror shining out her eyes, then with a low moan, bowed her head on her knees and shuddered, just as Lillian came in, curious to know what the handsome stranger had to say to her mother.

37 The poor mutilated body came home at last, and was laid in a stiff, silver-decorated, black coffin in the middle of the sitting-room, which had been made to look as uncomfortable and unnatural as mirrors and furniture shrouded in sheets and mantel and tables divested of ornaments would permit.

38 There was a wake that night to the unconfined joy of the neighbors, who would rather a burial than a wedding. The friends of the family sat about the coffin, and through the house with long pulled faces. Mrs. Tuckley officiated in the kitchen, making coffee and dispensing cheese and crackers to those who were hungry. As the night wore on, and the first restraint disappeared, jokes were cracked, and quiet laughter indulged in, while the young folks congregated in the kitchen, were hilariously happy, until some member of the family would appear, when every face would sober down.

39 The older persons contented themselves with recounting the virtues of the deceased, and telling anecdotes wherein he figured largely. It was astonishing how many intimate friends of his had suddenly come to light. Every other man present had either attended school with him, or was a close companion until he died. Proverbs and tales and witty sayings were palmed off as having emanated from his lips. In fact, the dead man would have been surprised

himself, had he suddenly come to life and discovered what an important, what a modern solomon he had become.

40 The long night dragged on, and the people departed in groups of twos and threes, until when the gray dawn crept slowly over the blackness of night shrouding the electric lights in mists of cloudy blue, and sending cold chills of dampness through the house, but a few of the great crowd remained.

41 The day seemed so gray in **contrast** to the softening influence of the night, the grief which could be hidden then, must now come forth and parade itself before all eyes. There was the funeral to prepare for; the dismal black dresses and bonnets with their long crape veils to don; there were the condolences of sorrowing friends to receive; the floral offerings to be looked at. The little Harts strutted about resplendent in stiff black cravats, and high crape bands about their hats. They were divided between two conflicting emotions—joy at belonging to a family so noteworthy and important, and sorrow at the death. As the time for the funeral approached, and Lillian began to indulge in a series of fainting fits, the latter feeling predominated.

42 Well it was all over at last, the family had returned, and as on two nights previous, sat once more in the deserted and dismantled parlor. Mrs. Tuckley and Mrs. Luke, having rendered all assistance possible, had repaired to their respective front steps to keep count of the number of visitors who returned to condole with the family.

43 "A real nice funeral," remarked the dress-maker at last, "a nice funeral. Everybody took it so hard, and Lillian fainted real beautiful. She's a good girl that Lillian. Poor things, I wonder what they'll do now."

44 Stella, the irrepressible, was busily engaged balancing herself on one toe, *a la* ballet.

45 "Mebbe she's goin' to get married," she volunteered eagerly, "'cos I saw that yeller-haired young man what comes there all the time, wif his arms around her waist, and a tellin' her not to grieve as he'd take care of her. I was a peepin' in the dinin'-room."

46 "How dare you peep at other folks, and pry into people's affairs? I can't imagine where you get your meddlesome ways from. There aint none in *my family*. Next time I catch you at it, I'll spank you good." Then, after a pause, "Well what else did he say?"

WRITE

LITERARY ANALYSIS: This story is built around two central events, a party and a wake. Write an essay analyzing the relationship between the party and the wake. What are the parallels between them? What are the differences? Why do you think the author chose to concentrate on these two events? Be sure to cite specific examples from the text to support your claims.

The Old Cabin

POETRY
Paul Laurence Dunbar
1905

Introduction

Paul Laurence Dunbar (1872–1906) was born and raised in Dayton, Ohio. His mother was a formerly enslaved person who learned how to read to support her son's education. Dunbar published poetry and fiction, as well as song lyrics for Broadway, and was one of the first African American poets to earn nationwide acclaim. As he does in this poem, Dunbar often experimented with writing in regional dialects along with conventional English. Dunbar expressed complicated feelings about writing in dialect. Although this dialect reflected his "natural speech," as he called it, he came to feel that writing in dialect biased white readers to African Americans. In this poem's original printing, "The Old Cabin" is accompanied by a series of black-and-white photographs depicting an African American woman in several scenes of life in slavery.

"I kin see de light a-shinin'"

> *Note: The text you are about to read contains offensive language. Remember to be mindful of the thoughts and feelings of your peers as you read and discuss this text. If needed, ask your teacher for additional guidance and support.*

1   In de dead of night I sometimes,
2   Git to t'inkin' of de pas'[1]
3   An' de days w'en slavery helt me
4   In my mis'ry—ha'd an' fas'.
5   Dough de time was mighty tryin',
6   In dese houahs somehow hit seem
7   Dat a brightah light come slippin'
8   Thoo de kivahs of my dream.

9   An' my min' fu'gits de whuppins
10   Draps de feah o' block an' lash
11   An' flies straight to somep'n' joyful
12   In a secon's lightnin' flash.
13   Den hit seems I see a **vision**
14   Of a dearah long ago
15   Of de childern tumblin' roun' me
16   By my rough ol' cabin do'.

---

1. **Git to t'inkin' of de pas'** Get to thinking about the past

17 Talk about yo' go'geous mansions
18 An' yo' big house great an' gran',
19 Des bring up de fines' palace
20 Dat you know in all de lan'.
21 But dey's somep'n' dearah to me,
22 Somep'n' **faihah** to my eyes
23 In dat cabin, less you bring me
24 To yo' mansion in de skies.

25 I kin see de light a-shinin'
26 Thoo de chinks atween de logs,
27 I kin hyeah de way-off **bayin'**
28 Of my mastah's huntin' dogs,
29 An' de neighin' of de hosses
30 Stampin' on de ol' bahn flo',
31 But above dese soun's de laughin'
32 At my deah ol' cabin do'.

33 We would gethah daih at evenin',
34 All my frien's 'ud come erroun'
35 An' hit wan't no time, twell, bless you,

36 You could hyeah de banjo's soun'.
37 You could see de dahkies dancin'
38 Pigeon wing[2] an' heel an' toe—
39 Joyous times I tell you people
40 Roun' dat same ol' cabin do'.

41 But at times my t'oughts gits saddah,
42 Ez I **riccolec'** de folks,
43 An' dey **frolickin'** an' talkin'
44 Wid dey laughin' an dey jokes.
45 An' hit hu'ts me w'en I membahs
46 Dat I'll nevah see no mo'
47 Dem ah faces gethered smilin'
48 Roun' dat po' ol' cabin do'.

2. **pigeon wing** an old-fashioned type of dance

 WRITE

RESEARCH: Poetry written during the Harlem Renaissance incorporated specific themes and references pertaining to African American history and culture. Research this literary focus. Then, write a literary analysis in which you investigate how "The Old Cabin"—written in 1905—prefigures some of the predominant themes and literary characteristics of the poetry of the Harlem Renaissance.

The Negro Speaks of Rivers

POETRY
Langston Hughes
1921

Introduction

One of American literature's most distinguished and innovative writers, Langston Hughes (1902–1967) was a prominent figure of the Harlem Renaissance in the early half of the 20th century. "The Negro Speaks of Rivers" was first published in *The Crisis*, the official magazine of the National Association for the Advancement of Colored People, or NAACP—edited at the time by W. E. B. Du Bois—when Hughes was just 20 years old. The poem remains one of Hughes's most famous. It is a stirring exploration of race and the human past, seen through the timeless and symbolic lens of the world's ancient rivers.

"My soul has grown deep like the rivers."

1   I've known rivers:
2   I've known rivers **ancient** as the world and older than the
3   flow of human blood in human veins.

4   My soul has grown deep like the rivers.

5   I bathed in the Euphrates[1] when dawns were young.
6   I built my hut near the Congo and it **lulled** me to sleep.
7   I looked upon the Nile and raised the pyramids above it.
8   I heard the singing of the Mississippi when Abe Lincoln
9   went down to New Orleans[2], and I've seen its **muddy**
10   **bosom** turn all golden in the sunset.

11 I've known rivers:
12 Ancient, **dusky** rivers.

13 My soul has grown deep like the rivers.

American poet and writer Langston Hughes,
c. 1945

---

1. **Euphrates** a river that flows from eastern Turkey through Syria and Iraq, bordering what was once Mesopotamia, the birthplace of human civilization
2. **Abe Lincoln / went down to New Orleans** When he was young, Abraham Lincoln twice sailed down the Mississippi River to New Orleans, his first exposure to the magnitude of the slave trade in 19th-century America.

WRITE

POETRY: Langston Hughes composed this poem when he had just graduated from high school, at the age of seventeen, while crossing the Mississippi River by train outside his hometown of St. Louis, Missouri. He was inspired by what he saw and his relationship to the landscape and its history. Think about a view that inspires you. Imagine you are looking out a particular window, at a particular landscape. Now write a poem about what you see and how it influences your sense of self and place. The landscape can be real or imagined but should be one to which you feel a connection. In your poem, mimic Hughes's use of repetition, historical and geographical references, and first-person point of view.

The Color of an Awkward Conversation

INFORMATIONAL TEXT
Chimamanda Ngozi Adichie
2008

Introduction

A bestselling author and winner of the National Book Critics Circle Award for her novel *Americanah*, Chimamanda Ngozi Adichie (b. 1977) has been described by *The New Yorker* as "a keen observer of American attitudes about race." The Nigerian native pursues her unique, humorous perspective on race in America in this essay.

"Still, what is most striking to me are the strange ways in which blackness is talked about."

1   I was annoyed the first time an African American man called me "sister." It was in a Brooklyn store, and I had recently arrived from Nigeria, a country where, thanks to the mosquitoes that kept British colonizers from settling, my skin color did not determine my identity, did not limit my dreams or my confidence. And so, although I grew up reading books about the **baffling** places where black people were treated badly for being black, race remained an exotic abstraction: It was Kunta Kinte[1].

2   Until that day in Brooklyn. To be called "sister" was to be black, and blackness was the very bottom of America's pecking order. I did not want to be black.

3   In college I babysat for a Jewish family, and once I went to pick up first-grader Stephen from his play date's home. The lovely house had an American flag hanging from a colonnade. The mother of Stephen's play date greeted me warmly. Stephen hugged me and went to look for his shoes. His play date ran down the stairs and stopped halfway. "She's black," he said to his mother and stared silently at me before going back upstairs. I laughed stupidly, perhaps to deflate the tension, but I was angry.

4   I was angry that this child did not merely think that black was different but had been taught that black was not a good thing. I was angry that his behavior left Stephen bewildered, and for a long time I half-expected something **similar** to happen in other homes that displayed American flags.

5   "That kid's mother is so ignorant," one friend said. "Ignorant" suggested that an **affluent**, educated American living in a Philadelphia suburb in 1999 did not realize that black people are human beings. "It was just a kid being a kid. It wasn't racist," another said. "Racist" suggested it was no big deal, since neither the child nor his mother had burned a cross in my yard. I called the first friend a Diminisher and the second a Denier and came to discover that both represented how mainstream America talks about blackness.

---

1. **Kunta Kinte** Protagonist of Alex Haley's 1976 novel *Roots: The Saga of an American Family*, Kunta Kinte is captured and transported from Africa into slavery in the American colonies.

6   Diminishers have a subtle intellectual superiority and depend on the word "ignorant." They believe that black people still encounter unpleasantness related to blackness but in **benign** forms and from unhappy people or crazy people or people with good intentions that are bungled in execution. Diminishers think that people can be "ignorant" but not "racist" because these people have black friends, supported the civil rights movements or had abolitionist forebears.

7   Deniers believe that black people stopped encountering unpleasantness related to their blackness when Martin Luther King Jr. died. They are "colorblind" and use expressions like "white, black or purple, we're all the same"—as though race were a biological rather than a social identity. Incidents that black people attribute to blackness are really about other factors, such as having too many children or driving too fast, but if deniers are compelled to accept that an incident was indeed about blackness, they launch into stories of Irish or Native American oppression, as though to deny the legitimacy of one story by generalizing about others. Deniers use "racist" as one would use "dinosaur," to refer to a phenomenon that no longer exists.

8   Although the way that blackness **manifests** itself in America has changed since 1965, the way that it is talked about has not. I have a great and complicated affection for this country—America is like my distant uncle who does not always remember my name but occasionally gives me pocket money—and what I admire most is its ability to create enduring myths. The myth of blackness is this: "Once upon a time, black towns were destroyed, black Americans were massacred and barred from voting, etc. All this happened because of racists. Today, these things no longer happen, and therefore racists no longer exist."

9   The word "racist" should be banned. It is like a sweater wrung completely out of shape; it has lost its usefulness. It makes honest debate impossible, whether about small realities such as little boys who won't say hello to black babysitters or large realities such as who is more likely to get the death penalty. In place of "racist," descriptive, albeit unwieldy, expressions might be used, such as "incidents that negatively affect black people, which, although possibly complicated by class and other factors, would not have occurred if the affected people were not black." Perhaps qualifiers would be added: "These incidents do not implicate all non-black people."

10   There are many stories like mine of Africans discovering blackness in America; of people who are consequently amused, resentful or puzzled by Americans being afraid of them or assuming they play sports or reacting to their intelligence with surprise. Still, what is most striking to me are the strange

NOTES

ways in which blackness is talked about. Ten years after first being called a "sister," I think of Don Cheadle as a talented brother, but I have never stopped being aware of the relative privilege of having had those West African mosquitoes.

Copyright @ 2008 by Chimamanda Ngozi Adichie, used by permission of The Wylie Agency LLC.

✏ WRITE

PERSONAL ESSAY: Chimamanda Ngozi Adichie has lived in both Nigeria and the United States and continues to split her time between both places, which gives her a unique vantage point from which to write about race. Choose a topic on which you have a unique vantage point, and write a personal essay that describes the topic and how you view it. Why is your perspective unique? How might your experience help others look at the topic in a different light?

How It Feels to Be Colored Me

INFORMATIONAL TEXT
Zora Neale Hurston
1928

Introduction

Zora Neale Hurston (1891–1960) was an African American writer and anthropologist who was one of the leading voices in the Harlem Renaissance. Although Hurston's preacher father sometimes sought to "squinch" her spirit, her mother urged young Zora and her seven siblings to "jump at de sun," and jump she did. Ten years before the publication of her most famous novel, *Their Eyes Were Watching God*, Hurston made her own declaration of independence with the autobiographical essay presented here, "How It Feels to Be Colored Me."

"I remember the very day that I became colored."

NOTES

1   I am colored but I offer nothing in the way of extenuating circumstances except the fact that I am the only Negro in the United States whose grandfather on the mother's side was *not* an Indian chief.

2   I remember the very day that I became colored. Up to my thirteenth year I lived in the little Negro town of Eatonville, Florida. It is exclusively a colored town. The only white people I knew passed through the town going to or coming from Orlando. The native whites rode dusty horses, the Northern tourists chugged down the sandy village road in automobiles. The town knew the Southerners and never stopped cane chewing when they passed. But the Northerners were something else again. They were peered at cautiously from behind curtains by the timid. The more venturesome would come out on the porch to watch them go past and got just as much pleasure out of the tourists as the tourists got out of the village.

3   The front porch might seem a daring place for the rest of the town, but it was a gallery seat for me. My favorite place was atop the gatepost. Proscenium box for a born first-nighter. Not only did I enjoy the show, but I didn't mind the actors knowing that I liked it. I usually spoke to them in passing. I'd wave at them and when they returned my salute, I would say something like this: "Howdy-do-well-I-thank-you-where-you-goin'?" Usually automobile or the horse paused at this, and after a queer exchange of compliments, I would probably "go a piece of the way" with them, as we say in farthest Florida. If one of my family happened to come to the front in time to see me, of course negotiations would be rudely broken off. But even so, it is clear that I was the first "welcome-to-our-state" Floridian, and I hope the Miami Chamber of Commerce will please take notice.

4   During this period, white people differed from colored to me only in that they rode through town and never lived there. They liked to hear me "speak pieces" and sing and wanted to see me dance the parse-me-la, and gave me generously of their small silver for doing these things, which seemed strange to me for I wanted to do them so much that I needed **bribing** to stop, only they didn't know it. The colored people gave no dimes. They **deplored** any

Skill: Author's Purpose and Point of View

Hurston explains that when she was a child white people treated her as if she existed for their entertainment. She wants to inform readers that, though African Americans didn't give her money, they gave her a place to belong.

NOTES

joyful tendencies in me, but I was their Zora nevertheless. I belonged to them, to the nearby hotels, to the county—everybody's Zora.

5   But changes came in the family when I was thirteen, and I was sent to school in Jacksonville. I left Eatonville, the town of the oleanders, a Zora. When I disembarked from the river-boat at Jacksonville, she was no more. It seemed that I had suffered a sea change. I was not Zora of Orange County any more, I was now a little colored girl. I found it out in certain ways. In my heart as well as in the mirror, I became a fast brown—warranted not to rub nor run.

6   But I am not tragically colored. There is no great sorrow dammed up in my soul, nor lurking behind my eyes. I do not mind at all. I do not belong to the sobbing school of Negrohood who hold that nature somehow has given them a lowdown dirty deal and whose feelings are all but about it. Even in the helter-skelter[1] skirmish that is my life, I have seen that the world is to the strong regardless of a little pigmentation more or less. No, I do not weep at the world—I am too busy sharpening my oyster knife.

7   Someone is always at my elbow reminding me that I am the granddaughter of slaves. It fails to register **depression** with me. Slavery is sixty years in the past. The operation was successful and the patient is doing well, thank you. The terrible struggle that made me an American out of a potential slave said "On the line!" The Reconstruction said "Get set!" and the generation before said "Go!" I am off to a flying start and I must not halt in the stretch to look behind and weep. Slavery is the price I paid for civilization, and the choice was not with me. It is a bully adventure and worth all that I have paid through my ancestors for it. No one on earth ever had a greater chance for glory. The world to be won and nothing to be lost. It is thrilling to think—to know that for any act of mine, I shall get twice as much praise or twice as much blame. It is quite exciting to hold the center of the national stage, with the spectators not knowing whether to laugh or to weep.

8   The position of my white neighbor is much more difficult. No brown specter pulls up a chair beside me when I sit down to eat. No dark ghost thrusts its leg against mine in bed. The game of keeping what one has is never so exciting as the game of getting.

9   I do not always feel colored. Even now I often achieve the unconscious Zora of Eatonville before the Hegira.[2] I feel most colored when I am thrown against a sharp white background.

 Skill: Figurative Language

This use of hyperbole emphasizes the author's enthusiasm and optimism at this point in her life. Again she uses a stage metaphor, but now she describes herself as being on center stage with the world as her audience.

---

1. **helter-skelter** in a disorderly or hasty manner
2. **Hegira** the journey of Muhammad and his followers from Mecca to Medina in the 7th century

NOTES

Skill: Central or
Main Idea

*As an adult, the author
is now more aware of
her race. She feels like
a dark rock, surrounded
by white people. She
feels her race and how
it impacts who she is,
but she is still able to be
herself.*

10   For instance at Barnard.[3] "Beside the waters of the Hudson" I feel my race. Among the thousand white persons, I am a dark rock surged upon, and overswept, but through it all, I remain myself. When covered by the waters, I am; and the ebb but reveals me again.

11   Sometimes it is the other way around. A white person is set down in our midst, but the contrast is just as sharp for me. For instance, when I sit in the drafty basement that is The New World Cabaret with a white person, my color comes. We enter chatting about any little nothing that we have in common and are seated by the jazz waiters. In the abrupt way that jazz orchestras have, this one plunges into a number. It loses no time in **circumlocutions,** but gets right down to business. It constricts the thorax and splits the heart with its tempo and narcotic harmonies. This orchestra grows rambunctious, rears on its hind legs and attacks the tonal veil with primitive fury, rending it, clawing it until it breaks through to the jungle beyond. I follow those heathen—follow them exultingly. I dance wildly inside myself; I yell within, I whoop; I shake my assegai above my head, I hurl it true to the mark *yeeeeooww!* I am in the jungle and living in the jungle way. My face is painted red and yellow and my body is painted blue. My pulse is throbbing like a war drum. I want to slaughter something—give pain, give death to what, I do not know. But the piece ends. The men of the orchestra wipe their lips and rest their fingers. I creep back slowly to the veneer we call civilization with the last tone and find the white friend sitting motionless in his seat, smoking calmly.

12   "Good music they have here," he remarks, drumming the table with his fingertips.

13   Music. The great blobs of purple and red emotion have not touched him. He has only heard what I felt. He is far away and I see him but dimly across the ocean and the continent that have fallen between us. He is so pale with his whiteness then and I am *so* colored.

14   At certain times I have no race, I am *me*. When I set my hat at a certain angle and saunter down Seventh Avenue, Harlem City, feeling as snooty as the lions in front of the Forty-Second Street Library, for instance. So far as my feelings are concerned, Peggy Hopkins Joyce[4] on the Boule Mich with her gorgeous raiment, stately carriage, knees knocking together in a most aristocratic manner, has nothing on me. The cosmic Zora emerges. I belong to no race nor time. I am the eternal feminine with its string of beads.

---

3. **Barnard** a liberal arts college in New York City
4. **Peggy Hopkins Joyce** an American model and actress known for leading a flamboyant, decadent lifestyle

15   I have no separate feeling about being an American citizen and colored. I am merely a fragment of the Great Soul that surges within the boundaries. My country, right or wrong.

16   Sometimes, I feel discriminated against, but it does not make me angry. It merely astonishes me. How *can* any deny themselves the pleasure of my company? It's beyond me.

17   But in the main, I feel like a brown bag of **miscellany** propped against a wall. Against a wall in company with other bags, white, red and yellow. Pour out the contents, and there is discovered a jumble of small things priceless and worthless. A first-water diamond, an empty spool, bits of broken glass, lengths of string, a key to a door long since crumbled away, a rusty knife-blade, old shoes saved for a road that never was and never will be, a nail bent under the weight of things too heavy for any nail, a dried flower or two still a little fragrant. In your hand is the brown bag. On the ground before you is the jumble it held—so much like the jumble in the bags, could they be emptied, that all might be dumped in a single heap and the bags refilled without altering the content of any greatly. A bit of colored glass more or less would not matter. Perhaps that is how the Great Stuffer of Bags filled them in the first place— who knows?

"How It Feels to Be Colored Me" from *I Love Myself When I Am Laughing* by Zora Neale Hurston. Published by The Feminist Press. Used by permission of The Permissions Company, Inc.

Please note that excerpts and passages in the StudySync® library and this workbook are intended as touchstones to generate interest in an author's work. The excerpts and passages do not substitute for the reading of entire texts, and StudySync® strongly recommends that students seek out and purchase the whole literary or informational work in order to experience it as the author intended. Links to online resellers are available in our digital library. In addition, complete works may be ordered through an authorized reseller by filling out and returning to StudySync® the order form enclosed in this workbook.

Reading & Writing Companion   **107**

First Read

Read "How It Feels to Be Colored Me." After you read, complete the Think Questions below.

1. How is life in Jacksonville different for Zora than it was in Eatonville? What are the significant changes, and how do they affect her? Cite evidence from the text to support your answer.

2. Why doesn't being the granddaughter of slaves "register depression" in Zora? Summarize Hurston's position on this part of her cultural history, quoting passages from the text to support your response.

3. What does Hurston's anecdote about the New World Cabaret convey to readers? Why does she share this story? Use evidence from the text to support your response.

4. What does the verb **deplored** mean as it appears in the text? Write your best definition of *deplored* here, along with a brief explanation of how you arrived at its meaning.

5. The Latin root *circum* means "around." With this in mind, what context clues helped you determine the meaning of **circumlocutions** as it appears in the text?

Skill:
Central or Main Idea

Use the Checklist to analyze Central or Main Idea in "How It Feels to Be Colored Me." Refer to the sample student annotation about Central or Main Idea in the text.

••• CHECKLIST FOR CENTRAL OR MAIN IDEA

In order to identify two or more central ideas of a text, note the following:

- ✓ the main idea in each paragraph or group of paragraphs

- ✓ key details in each paragraph or section of text, distinguishing what they have in common

- ✓ whether the details contain information that could indicate more than one main idea in a text

  - • a science text, for example, may provide information about a specific environment and also a message on ecological awareness

  - • a biography may contain equally important ideas about a person's achievements, influence, and the time period in which the person lives or lived

- ✓ when each central idea emerges

- ✓ ways that the central ideas interact and build on one another

To determine two or more central ideas of a text and analyze their development over the course of the text, including how they interact and build on one another to provide a complex analysis, consider the following questions:

- ✓ What main idea(s) do the details in each paragraphs explain or describe?

- ✓ What central or main ideas do all the paragraphs support?

- ✓ How do the central ideas interact and build on one another? How does that affect when they emerge?

- ✓ How might you provide an objective summary of the text? What details would you include?

Skill:
Central or Main Idea

Reread paragraphs 15–17 of "How It Feels to Be Colored Me." Then, using the Checklist on the previous page, answer the multiple-choice questions below.

⟳ YOUR TURN

1. This question has two parts. First, answer Part A. Then, answer Part B.

   Part A: What is the main idea of the final paragraph of the essay?

   ○ A. Despite differing appearances on the exterior, all human beings are quite similar on the inside.

   ○ B. The author does not feel threatened by people of other races.

   ○ C. It does not matter what color you are because all human beings are worthy of respect.

   ○ D. There are many random things that make us who we are.

   Part B: Which line from the passage provides the best evidence to your answer in Part A?

   ○ A. ". . . old shoes saved for a road that never was and never will be, a nail bent under the weight of things too heavy for any nail, a dried flower or two still a little fragrant."

   ○ B. "Against a wall in company with other bags, white, red and yellow."

   ○ C. "Pour out the contents, and there is discovered a jumble of small things priceless and worthless."

   ○ D. ". . . could they be emptied, that all might be dumped in a single heap and the bags refilled without altering the content of any greatly."

Skill:
Figurative Language

Use the Checklist to analyze Figurative Language in "How It Feels to Be Colored Me." Refer to the sample student annotation about Figurative Language in the text.

••• CHECKLIST FOR FIGURATIVE LANGUAGE

In order to determine the meaning of figurative language in context, note the following:

- ✓ words that mean one thing literally and suggest something else

- ✓ figures of speech, including metaphors and similes

- ✓ figures of speech, including hyperbole, or exaggerated statements not meant to be taken literally, such as:

  - a child saying, "I'll be doing this homework until I'm 100!"

  - a claim such as "I'm so hungry I could eat a horse!"

In order to interpret figurative language in context and analyze its role in the text, consider the following questions:

- ✓ Where is there figurative language in the text, and what seems to be the purpose of the author's use of it?

- ✓ Why does the author use a figure of speech rather than literal language?

- ✓ What impact do similes, metaphors, or hyperbole have on your understanding of the text?

- ✓ How does the figurative language develop the message or theme of the text?

Please note that excerpts and passages in the StudySync® library and this workbook are intended as touchstones to generate interest in an author's work. The excerpts and passages do not substitute for the reading of entire texts, and StudySync® strongly recommends that students seek out and purchase the whole literary or informational work in order to experience it as the author intended. Links to online resellers are available in our digital library. In addition, complete works may be ordered through an authorized reseller by filling out and returning to StudySync® the order form enclosed in this workbook.

Reading & Writing Companion   **111**

Skill:
Figurative Language

Reread paragraph 11 of "How It Feels to Be Colored Me." Then, using the Checklist on the previous page, answer the multiple-choice questions below.

⟳ YOUR TURN

1. Figurative language such as "rears on its hind legs" and "throbbing like a war drum" suggests what about the author's reaction to the music?

   ○ A. The figurative language shows that the music makes the author very anxious.

   ○ B. The figurative language shows that the author very much dislikes the music.

   ○ C. The figurative language shows that the music brings out something animalistic in the author.

   ○ D. The figurative language shows that different people have different reactions to music.

2. What is the intended effect of the author's hyperbolic descriptions of her actions while listening to the music?

   ○ A. They are intended to illustrate the stark contrast between her reaction to the music and that of her white companion.

   ○ B. They are intended to illustrate the intense personal connection that the author has to jazz music because of where she comes from.

   ○ C. They are intended to illustrate how negative a reaction the author has to the music.

   ○ D. They are intended to illustrate for the reader how music plays an important role in the author's adult life.

Skill: Author's Purpose and Point of View

Use the Checklist to analyze Author's Purpose and Point of View in "How It Feels to Be Colored Me." Refer to the sample student annotation about Author's Purpose and Point of View in the text.

••• CHECKLIST FOR AUTHOR'S PURPOSE AND POINT OF VIEW

In order to identify author's purpose and point of view, note the following:

- ✓ whether the writer is attempting to establish trust by citing his or her experience or education

- ✓ whether the evidence the author provides is convincing and the argument or position is logical

- ✓ what words and phrases the author uses to appeal to the emotions

- ✓ the author's use of rhetoric, or the art of speaking and writing persuasively, such as the use of repetition to drive home a point, as well as allusion and alliteration

- ✓ the author's use of rhetoric to contribute to the power, persuasiveness, or beauty of the text

To determine the author's purpose and point of view, consider the following questions:

- ✓ How does the author try to convince me that he or she has something valid and important for me to read?

- ✓ What words or phrases express emotion or invite an emotional response? How or why are they effective or ineffective?

- ✓ What words and phrases contribute to the power, persuasiveness, or beauty of the text? Is the author's use of rhetoric successful? Why or why not?

Please note that excerpts and passages in the StudySync® library and this workbook are intended as touchstones to generate interest in an author's work. The excerpts and passages do not substitute for the reading of entire texts, and StudySync® strongly recommends that students seek out and purchase the whole literary or informational work in order to experience it as the author intended. Links to online resellers are available in our digital library. In addition, complete works may be ordered through an authorized reseller by filling out and returning to StudySync® the order form enclosed in this workbook.

Reading & Writing Companion   **113**

Skill: Author's Purpose and Point of View

Reread paragraph 17 of "How It Feels to Be Colored Me." Then, using the Checklist on the previous page, answer the multiple-choice questions below.

↻ YOUR TURN

1. Which of the following sentences **best** describes the purpose the author wants to achieve regarding her audience in this paragraph?

   ○ A. Hurston wants her audience to recognize that their lives are random and simplistic.

   ○ B. Hurston wants to show her audience that individual lives are just a random jumble of ideas that mean very little.

   ○ C. Hurston wants to persuade her audience to see that we're all similar on the inside and that is what matters.

   ○ D. Hurston wants the audience to share her view that every object in the world is "a fragment of the Great Soul."

2. What point of view is the author imparting in this passage?

   ○ A. Racism is the result of economic injustice.

   ○ B. People should share and then redistribute their wealth.

   ○ C. Race is not an indicator of worth or value.

   ○ D. People who are alike on the inside get mistreated because of race.

Close Read

Reread "How It Feels to Be Colored Me" and "The Negro Speaks of Rivers." As you reread, complete the Skills Focus questions below. Then use your answers and annotations from the questions to help you complete the Write activity.

⊙ SKILLS FOCUS

1. Analyze context, including imagery, to help you determine the nuanced meaning of the word *fast* in paragraph 5. Explain how context clues helped you understand the word's meaning.

2. Highlight an example of how Hurston uses figurative language. Explain how such rhetorical devices affect your reading experience and your understanding the text.

3. Identify an example in which Hurston seems to be encouraging herself to stand strong against the tide of racial difference. What main idea is she communicating to the reader? Analyze how addressing a dual audience deepens the meaning of the text.

4. Find an example of when Hurston feels least confined by perceptions of race as an adult. Analyze how the author's description of herself in this example relates to her purpose and point of view.

5. Hurston's experiences deepened her understanding of the intersection of ideology and identity. How might Hurston's outlook on her identity have been different if she had never left home? Highlight evidence from the text to support your answer.

✎ WRITE

DISCUSSION: The texts "The Negro Speaks of Rivers," "How It Feels to Be Colored Me," and the more contemporary "The Color of an Awkward Conversation" provide insight into the authors' various perspectives about race and society. What are the messages of these texts, and are they expressed effectively? Determine the message of each text and then describe to what extent figurative language strengthens the messages, using relevant evidence from the text.

Please note that excerpts and passages in the StudySync® library and this workbook are intended as touchstones to generate interest in an author's work. The excerpts and passages do not substitute for the reading of entire texts, and StudySync® strongly recommends that students seek out and purchase the whole literary or informational work in order to experience it as the author intended. Links to online resellers are available in our digital library. In addition, complete works may be ordered through an authorized reseller by filling out and returning to StudySync® the order form enclosed in this workbook.

Reading & Writing Companion 115

Invisible Man

FICTION
Ralph Ellison
1952

Introduction

Winner of the 1953 National Book Award, *Invisible Man* by Ralph Ellison (1914–1994) confronts the social, intellectual, and psychological consequences of living as a black man in America. The unnamed protagonist, who lives rent-free in the forgotten basement of a whites-only apartment on the outskirts of Harlem, tells his life story including his education at Tuskegee, his employment at Liberty Paints in Harlem, and his involvement in a Marxist interracial organization called The Brotherhood. *Invisible Man* is noteworthy not only for its commentary on American race relations but also for its experimental structure, Modernist use of symbolism, stream-of-consciousness narration, and biting satire.

". . . and I might even be said to possess a mind."

From The Prologue

1   I am an invisible man. No, I am not a spook like those who haunted Edgar Allan Poe; nor am I one of your Hollywood-movie **ectoplasms**. I am a man of substance, of flesh and bone, fiber and liquids—and I might even be said to possess a mind. I am invisible, understand, simply because people refuse to see me. Like the bodiless heads you see sometimes in circus sideshows,[1] it is as though I have been surrounded by mirrors of hard, distorting glass. When they approach me they see only my surroundings, themselves, or figments of their imagination—indeed, everything and anything except me.

2   Nor is my invisibility exactly a matter of a bio-chemical accident to my **epidermis**. That invisibility to which I refer occurs because of a peculiar disposition of the eyes of those with whom I come in contact. A matter of the construction of their inner eyes, those eyes with which they look through their physical eyes upon reality. I am not complaining, nor am I protesting either. It is sometimes advantageous to be unseen, although it is most often rather wearing on the nerves. Then too, you're constantly being bumped against by those of poor vision. Or again, you often doubt if you really exist. You wonder whether you aren't simply a phantom in other people's minds. Say, a figure in a nightmare which the sleeper tries with all his strength to destroy. It's when you feel like this that, out of resentment, you begin to bump people back. And, let me confess, you feel that way most of the time. You ache with the need to convince yourself that you do exist in the real world, that you're a part of all the sound and anguish, and you strike out with your fists, you curse and you swear to make them recognize you. And, alas, it's seldom successful.

3   One night I accidentally bumped into a man, and perhaps because of the near darkness he saw me and called me an insulting name. I sprang at him, seized his coat lapels and demanded that he apologize. He was a tall blond man, and as my face came close to his he looked **insolently** out of his blue eyes and cursed me, his breath hot in my face as he struggled. I pulled his chin down sharp upon the crown of my head, butting him as I had seen the

Skill:
Textual Evidence

Reading the text closely, it seems that the narrator has become resentful at feeling invisible, causing him to respond with violence in order to be recognized, even though this isn't often effective.

---

1. **sideshow** an old-fashioned traveling circus featuring games and sensationalized attractions

West Indians do, and I felt his flesh tear and the blood gush out, and I yelled, "Apologize! Apologize!" But he continued to curse and struggle, and I butted him again and again until he went down heavily, on his knees, **profusely** bleeding. I kicked him repeatedly, in a frenzy because he still uttered insults though his lips were frothy with blood. Oh yes, I kicked him! And in my outrage I got out my knife and prepared to slit his throat, right there beneath the lamplight in the deserted street, holding him by the collar with one hand, and opening the knife with my teeth—when it occurred to me that the man had not seen me, actually; that he, as far as he knew, was in the midst of a walking nightmare! And I stopped the blade, slicing the air as I pushed him away, letting him fall back to the street. I stared at him hard as the lights of a car stabbed through the darkness. He lay there, moaning on the asphalt; a man almost killed by a phantom. It unnerved me. I was both disgusted and ashamed. I was like a drunken man myself, wavering about on weakened legs. Then I was amused. Something in this man's thick head had sprung out and beaten him within an inch of his life. I began to laugh at this crazy discovery. Would he have awakened at the point of death? Would Death himself have freed him for wakeful living? But I didn't linger. I ran away into the dark, laughing so hard I feared I might rupture myself. The next day I saw his picture in the Daily News, beneath a caption stating that he had been "mugged." Poor fool, poor blind fool, I thought with sincere compassion, mugged by an invisible man!

4   Most of the time (although I do not choose as I once did to deny the violence of my days by ignoring it) I am not so overtly violent. I remember that I am invisible and walk softly so as not to awaken the sleeping ones. Sometimes it is best not to awaken them; there are few things in the world as dangerous as sleepwalkers. I learned in time though that it is possible to carry on a fight against them without their realizing it. For instance, I have been carrying on a fight with Monopolated Light & Power for some time now. I use their service and pay them nothing at all, and they don't know it. Oh, they suspect that power is being drained off, but they don't know where. All they know is that according to the master meter back there in their power station a hell of a lot of free current is disappearing somewhere into the jungle of Harlem. The joke, of course, is that I don't live in Harlem but in a border area. Several years ago (before I discovered the advantage of being invisible) I went through the routine process of buying service and paying their outrageous rates. But no more. I gave up all that, along with my apartment, and my old way of life: That way based upon the **fallacious** assumption that I, like other men, was visible. Now, aware of my invisibility, I live rent-free in a building rented strictly to whites, in a section of the basement that was shut off and forgotten during the nineteenth century, which I discovered when I was trying to escape in the night from Ras the Destroyer. But that's getting too far ahead of the story, almost to the end, although the end is in the beginning and lies far ahead.

5   The point now is that I found a home—or a hole in the ground, as you will. Now don't jump to the conclusion that because I call my home a "hole" it is damp and cold like a grave; there are cold holes and warm holes. Mine is a warm hole. And remember, a bear retires to his hole for the winter and lives until spring; then he comes strolling out like the Easter chick breaking from its shell. I say all this to assure you that it is incorrect to assume that, because I'm invisible and live in a hole, I am dead. I am neither dead nor in a state of suspended animation. Call me Jack-the-Bear,[2] for I am in a state of hibernation.

6   My hole is warm and full of light. Yes, full of light. I doubt if there is a brighter spot in all New York than this hole of mine, and I do not exclude Broadway. Or the Empire State Building on a photographer's dream night. But that is taking advantage of you. Those two spots are among the darkest of our whole civilization—pardon me, our whole culture (an important distinction, I've heard)—which might sound like a hoax, or a contradiction, but that (by contradiction, I mean) is how the world moves: Not like an arrow, but a boomerang. (Beware of those who speak of the spiral of history; they are preparing a boomerang. Keep a steel helmet handy.)

7   I know; I have been boomeranged across my head so much that I now can see the darkness of lightness. And I love light. Perhaps you'll think it strange that an invisible man should need light, desire light, love light. But maybe it is exactly because I am invisible. Light confirms my reality, gives birth to my form.

Excerpted from *Invisible Man* by Ralph Ellison, published by Vintage International.

---

2. **Jack-the-Bear** a trickster figure from Southern folk stories of anthropomorphized animals

First Read

Read *Invisible Man*. After you read, complete the Think Questions below.

 THINK QUESTIONS

1. According to the narrator, what are some advantages of invisibility? Cite specific evidence from the text to support your answer.

2. What does the protagonist mean when he says he wants to "bump people back," and why? Cite evidence from the text in support of your answer.

3. Where does the narrator live and how does he describe his living space? Point to evidence from the text to support your answer.

4. Use context clues to determine the meaning of the word **epidermis** as it is used in *Invisible Man*, and write your best definition of the word here. Describe which clues led you to your answer.

5. Use context clues to determine the meaning of the word **fallacious** as it is used in *Invisible Man*. Write your definition of *fallacious* here and explain how you figured out its meaning.

Skill:
Textual Evidence

Use the Checklist to analyze Textual Evidence in *Invisible Man*. Refer to the sample student annotations about Textual Evidence in the text.

••• CHECKLIST FOR TEXTUAL EVIDENCE

In order to support an analysis by citing evidence that is explicitly stated in the text, do the following:

✓ read the text closely and critically

✓ identify what the text says explicitly

✓ find the most relevant textual evidence that supports your analysis

✓ consider why an author explicitly states specific details and information

✓ cite the specific words, phrases, sentences, or paragraphs from the text that support your analysis

✓ determine where evidence in the text still leaves certain matters uncertain or unresolved

In order to interpret implicit meanings in a text by making inferences, do the following:

✓ combine information directly stated in the text with your own knowledge, experiences, and observations

✓ cite the specific words, phrases, sentences, or paragraphs from the text that led to and support this inference

In order to cite textual evidence to support an analysis of what the text says explicitly as well as inferences drawn from the text, consider the following questions:

✓ Have I read the text closely and critically?

✓ What inferences am I making about the text?

✓ What textual evidence am I using to support these inferences?

✓ Am I quoting the evidence from the text correctly?

✓ Does my textual evidence logically relate to my analysis or the inference I am making?

✓ Does evidence in the text still leave certain matters unanswered or unresolved? In what ways?

Skill:
Textual Evidence

Reread paragraph 4 of *Invisible Man*. Then, using the Checklist on the previous page, answer the multiple-choice questions below.

⟳ YOUR TURN

1. This question has two parts. First, answer Part A. Then, answer Part B.

   Part A: Identify an inference based on evidence from the passage.

   ○ A. The sleeping ones, or sleepwalkers, are the white people who refuse to see him.

   ○ B. The narrator does not like where he lives.

   ○ C. The narrator used to work for Monopolated Light & Power.

   ○ D. The narrator thinks that he pays too much for electricity.

   Part B: Which sentence supports your answer to the question in Part A?

   ○ A. "All they know is that according to the master meter back there in their power station a hell of a lot of free current is disappearing somewhere into the jungle of Harlem."

   ○ B. "Now, aware of my invisibility, I live rent-free in a building rented strictly to whites, in a section of the basement that was shut off and forgotten during the nineteenth century . . . "

   ○ C. "But no more. I gave up all that, along with my apartment, and my old way of life: That way based upon the **fallacious** assumption that I, like other men, was visible."

   ○ D. "But that's getting too far ahead of the story, almost to the end, although the end is in the beginning and lies far ahead."

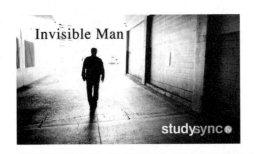

Close Read

Reread *Invisible Man*. As you reread, complete the Skills Focus questions below. Then use your answers and annotations from the questions to help you complete the Write activity.

◎ SKILLS FOCUS

1. Identify evidence that demonstrates the ways the protagonist is invisible. Explain how the evidence from the text you've chosen addresses your reasoning.

2. Reread paragraph 3 and use context clues to determine the meaning of the word **insolent**. Highlight the clues that help you determine the word's meaning, and annotate with your best definition of the word.

3. Explain how ideologies, either the narrator's or others', affect the narrator's life. Identify evidence from the text to support your response.

✏ WRITE

LITERARY ANALYSIS: In the excerpt from *Invisible Man*, the narrator reflects on his identity in a world that does not see him. In a written response, analyze the narrator's representation of his invisibility and make an argument about how that invisibility profoundly impacts the narrator's interactions with others. Support your response with evidence from the text.

Please note that excerpts and passages in the StudySync® library and this workbook are intended as touchstones to generate interest in an author's work. The excerpts and passages do not substitute for the reading of entire texts, and StudySync® strongly recommends that students seek out and purchase the whole literary or informational work in order to experience it as the author intended. Links to online resellers are available in our digital library. In addition, complete works may be ordered through an authorized reseller by filling out and returning to StudySync® the order form enclosed in this workbook.

Reading & Writing Companion   **123**

Extended Writing Project and Grammar

EXTENDED WRITING PROJECT
RESEARCH WRITING

RESEARCH
WRITING
PROCESS
PLAN

Research Writing Process: Plan

PLAN	DRAFT	REVISE	EDIT AND PUBLISH

The Harlem Renaissance was a period when African American art and culture began to flourish in mainstream American culture. Poets, musicians, artists, and writers sought to define and explore the African American experience on African American terms. What emerged was a proliferation of work that examined the influence of slavery on the lives of black Americans, brought attention to African American folklore, introduced a context in which to describe black urban life in the North, addressed the impacts of discrimination, and celebrated African American culture at large. By bringing these issues into the American cultural mainstream, the Harlem Renaissance also laid the groundwork for the burgeoning civil rights movement of the 1940s and 1950s.

WRITING PROMPT

What role do art and culture have in bringing awareness to social issues?

Choose one to two artists or writers, not included in this unit, from the Harlem Renaissance whom you would like to research. For example, you might research a writer who was born in the South but moved to a Northern city, such as Richard Wright. You might choose to focus on the early life of writer Claude McKay, the career of Paul Robeson, or the success of Ma Rainey. Research your chosen topic, and formulate a position on how your subjects' work contributed to gaining greater visibility for African Americans in mainstream culture, how the work impacted society, or how your subjects' life experiences impacted their work. Then, write an informative research essay, using textual evidence and source material to support your ideas. Be sure your informative research paper includes the following:

- an introduction
- supporting details from at least three credible sources
- a clear text structure
- a conclusion
- a works cited page

Writing to Sources

As you gather ideas and information from sources, be sure to:

- use evidence from multiple sources, and
- avoid overly relying on one source.

Introduction to Informative Research Writing

Research writing, a type of informative writing, examines a topic and conveys ideas by citing and analyzing information from credible sources. Good research papers use textual evidence, including facts, statistics, examples, and details from reliable sources, to provide information about a topic and to support the analysis of complex ideas. Research helps writers not only to discover and confirm facts but also to draw new conclusions about a topic. The characteristics of research writing include:

- an introduction with a clear thesis statement

- relevant facts, supporting details, and quotations from credible sources

- analysis of the details to explain how they support the thesis

- a clear and logical text structure

- a formal style

- a conclusion that wraps up your ideas

- a works cited page

In addition to these characteristics, writers also carefully narrow the focus of their research by generating research questions and developing a research plan. The research process requires patience as you evaluate the validity and usefulness of sources related to your topic. Researchers develop the skills of locating sources and assessing their appropriateness over time.

As you continue with this Extended Writing Project, you'll receive more instruction and practice in crafting each of the characteristics of informative research writing to create your own research paper.

Before you get started on your own informative research paper, read this research paper that one student, Daniela, wrote in response to the writing prompt. As you read the Model, highlight and annotate the features of informative research writing that Daniela included in her essay.

Post-Reconstruction Blues:

How Gertrude "Ma" Rainey Sang Black Rural Southerners into Popular American Culture

1   Legendary blues vocalist and Harlem Renaissance artist Gertrude "Ma" Rainey, known as the "Mother of Blues," introduced blues music to a mainstream audience, transforming the genre and expanding opportunities for African American artists. Through lyrical depictions of black Southern life and the complex experiences of African American women, Rainey's music increased the visibility of a people silenced in popular culture. While less well-known today, Rainey left a legacy that continues to influence musicians and broaden our knowledge of life for African Americans in the post-Reconstruction era.

2   Ma Rainey was born Gertrude Malissa Nix Pridgett on April 26, 1886, in Columbus, Georgia. Rainey possessed a musical talent from a young age and performed in public for the first time at age 14 at the Springer Opera House in Columbus. Soon after, she found her calling singing on tour in vaudeville and African American minstrel shows. For more than thirty years, Rainey performed in troupes, such as F.S. Wolcott's Rabbit Foot Minstrels and Tolliver's Circus and Musical Extravaganza.

Vaudeville: Ma Rainey's Early Career

3   Ma Rainey used vaudeville and minstrel shows as a platform to showcase her talent and share her life experiences. Originating from minstrel shows, vaudeville became popular at the turn of the century and featured unrelated acts such as singing, dancing, comedy, acrobatics, and magic. While no video recordings of Ma Rainey exist, the memory of her vibrant performances has been passed down through written reviews. According to critic Mary L. Bogumil in *Understanding August Wilson*, Rainey wore "flamboyant" jewelry and costumes and performed in front of a backdrop that featured a

NOTES

large gramophone design, "which gave the appearance of Ma emerging right from the speaker, issuing from and manifesting the music itself" (qtd. in Timmel). Such extravagant details exemplify the sensational nature of vaudeville shows. Rainey's bold and brilliant stage persona was magnetic. She forced the audience, who were often men, to listen to what she had to say.

4   The variety show format of vaudeville allowed performers to communicate larger themes to the audience. For example, PBS's *American Masters* says of immigrant performers, "Their acts were a form of assimilation, in which they could become active parts of popular culture through representations of their heritage" ("Vaudeville: About Vaudeville"). In other words, immigrant performers used the highly adaptable and entertaining structure of vaudeville to disseminate information about where they came from. Ma Rainey was not an immigrant. However, as an African American woman, she belonged to a class of citizens who were underrepresented, misunderstood, and discriminated against. Like the immigrants, she used the modes of performance available to her to subvert boundaries and bring the experiences of Southern African American women into the mainstream ("Vaudeville: About Vaudeville"). That Ma Rainey was also the first woman to include blues music in her act only further illustrates her ability to use this mode of performance to break barriers and convey an important message (Orr).

The Blues: Ma Rainey's Medium

5   The blues played a central part in Rainey's performances. Originating in the South at the turn of the century, blues emerged from such African musical traditions as field hollers, work songs, spirituals, and country string ballads ("What Is the Blues?"). Most blues songs follow a 12-bar structure with an AAB verse pattern where "the first and second lines are repeated, and the third line is a response to them—often with a twist" ("Understanding the 12-Bar Blues"). Blues music tends to explore melancholy topics, such as sadness, desire, and longing. While many of Rainey's songs had a melancholy tone, her music also served to empower women by approaching topics most women could not discuss freely.

6   Ma Rainey's audience easily connected to her songs because her lyrics discussed aspects of everyday life for black rural Southerners as well as her personal experiences. According to William Barlow in *Looking Up at Down*, Rainey's lyrics captured "the southern landscape of African Americans in the Post-Reconstruction era" through "simple, straightforward stories" (qtd. in Biography.com Editors). For example, in 1923, Rainey recorded her own rendition of the traditional boll weevil song, titled "Bo Weavil Blues." In the first verse, she sang, "Bo-weavil, don't sing them blues no more / Bo-weavil's here, bo-weavil's everywhere you'll go." A boll weevil is a type of beetle that feeds on cotton plants. Because boll weevils infested cotton crops in the United States in the 1920s, this lyric reflected rural Southern life at the time. Rainey established a call-and-response structure between the first and second verses as she sang, "I'm a lone bo-weavil, been out a great long time / I'm gonna sing these blues to ease the bo-weavil's lonesome mind." Here, she expanded the boll weevil reference to her personal life. Although there were boll weevils "everywhere you'll go," she still felt "lonesome." Boll weevils represented all the men, or potential romantic partners, available to her.

7   Ma Rainey's candid discussion of love was unique to blues artists of her time. She was lonely but also embraced her independence ("I don't want no man to put sugar in my tea."). Rainey's rejection of a male partner was radical, for women in this time period were expected to build their lives around being married and having a family. In *Blues Legacies* and *Black Feminism*, Angela Davis pointed out that "black women of that era were acknowledging and addressing issues central to contemporary feminist discourse" (Davis 28). Black female blues artists like Ma Rainey were ahead of

their time in terms of asserting their agency. Rainey's performance of this song introduced the idea of liberated black women into the mainstream. Rainey added complexity to this with a twist in the third verse:

> I went downtown and bought me a hat
> I brought it back home, I laid it on the shelf
> Looked at my bed, I'm getting tired of sleeping by myself (Rainey)

8   Ma Rainey used straightforward phrases to explain how she tried to compensate for her loneliness by purchasing a hat, but it did not help. The expression "tired of sleeping" emphasized her internal conflict. Sleep is the solution for tiredness, just as a relationship should have been the solution for her loneliness. Yet, Rainey preferred her independence. In only twelve lines, she referenced a regional metaphor, discussed the relatable concept of loneliness, and expressed her personal struggles balancing love and freedom.

Ma Rainey and the Mainstream Music Industry

9   Rainey's vocals had a deep and unembellished tone expressing raw emotion that resonated with a wide range of audiences. "The gravelly timbre of her . . . raspy, deep voice" (Orr) as well as her "moaning style" (Timmel) entranced listeners. Her flashy visual representation attracted the attention of the audience. Her measured and gripping delivery kept them waiting for more. Ma Rainey was one of the first professional female blues artists to make a phonograph record. During the Great Migration, blues music spread from the South into other regions of the nation.

THE GREAT MIGRATION
The Migration of African Americans from the American South (1910 - 1970)

By the 1920s, recording labels saw a market for "race records," or music created by and for African Americans. After establishing her career as a touring musician, Ma Rainey recorded over 100 songs with Paramount in the span of 1923 to 1928 (Timmel). However, in 1928 Paramount stopped recording with Rainey after determining that race records like hers were no longer profitable. One could argue that Paramount exploited Ma Rainey for corporate gain. Still, making a phonograph record with Paramount did help Rainey's audience and success grow. Over the course of her career, she performed alongside various bands and other renowned Harlem Renaissance musicians, such as Louis Armstrong and Bessie Smith.

10   In an era when the possibilities for women of color were limited, the "Mother of Blues," Ma Rainey, surpassed expectations by taking advantage of the modes of performance that were available to her to build a long-lasting career. Rainey used the public platforms of vaudeville and recorded music to tell the stories of Southern African Americans during the post-Reconstruction Era. Her lyrics also revealed her own stories and sentiments that are unique to the experiences of black women at that time. Her deeply emotional vocal style appealed to many people. Ma Rainey's blues music demanded recognition through simple portrayals of authenticity. She brought the silenced narratives of African Americans into the scope of mainstream American culture.

Works Cited

Biography.com Editors. "Ma Rainey Biography." *The Biography.com Website*, A&E Television Networks, 27 Apr. 2017, https://www.biography.com/people/ma-rainey-9542413. Accessed 20 Sept. 2018.

Davis, Angela Y. *Blues Legacies and Black Feminism: Gertrude "Ma" Rainey, Bessie Smith, and Billie Holiday. Google Books*. 2nd ed., Vintage Books, 1999.

Orr, N. Lee. "Gertrude 'Ma' Rainey (1886-1939)." 9 May 2003. *New Georgia Encyclopedia*, Georgia State University, 9 Aug. 2018, https://www.georgiaencyclopedia.org/articles/arts-culture/gertrude-ma-rainey-1886–1939. Accessed 20 Sep. 2018.

Rainey, Ma. "Bo-Weavil Blues." *Harry's Blues Lyrics & Tabs Online*, Recorded December 1923, http://blueslyrics.tripod.com/lyrics/ma rainey/bo weavil blues.htm. Accessed 25 Sep. 2018.

Timmel, Lisa. "The Music of Ma Rainey." *Huntington Theater Company*, https://www.huntingtontheatre.org/articles/Ma-Raineys-Black-Bottom/music-ma-rainey/. Accessed 20 Sep. 2018.

"The Great Migration, 1910 to 1970." The United States Census Bureau, September 13, 2012, https://www.census.gov/dataviz/visualizations/020/. Sep. 2018.

"Understanding the 12-Bar Blues." *PBS: The Blues*, 2003, www.pbs.org/theblues/classroom/essays12bar.html. Accessed 21 Sep. 2018.

"Vaudeville: About Vaudeville." *PBS: American Masters*, 8 Oct. 1999, www.pbs.org/wnet/americanmasters/vaudeville-about-vaudeville/721/. Accessed 20 Sept. 2018.

"What Is the Blues?" *PBS: The Blues*, 2003, www.pbs.org/theblues/classroom/essaysblues.html. Accessed 21 Sep. 2018.

✏ WRITE

Writers often take notes about ideas before they sit down to write. Think about what you've learned so far about organizing informative research writing to help you begin prewriting.

- **Purpose:** Which Harlem Renaissance writer or artist do you find most influential? What do you want to learn about your chosen subject?
- **Audience:** Who is your audience, and what information do you want your audience to learn?
- **Questions:** How can you use a research question to focus your research?
- **Sources:** What kinds of sources will help you answer that question?
- **Structure:** How can you share the information you find with readers?

Response Instructions

Use the questions in the bulleted list to write a one-paragraph research summary. Your summary should describe what you plan to research and discuss in this research paper. Include possible research questions of your own based on the prompt.

Don't worry about including all of the details now; focus only on the most essential and important elements. You will refer to this short summary as you continue through the steps of the writing process.

Skill:
Planning Research

In order to conduct a short or more sustained research project to answer a question or solve a problem, do the following:

- select a topic or problem to research

- think about what you want to find out and what kind of research can contribute to the project

- start to formulate your major research question by asking open-ended questions that begin "How . . .?" and "Why . . . ?" and then choose a question that you are interested in exploring

- narrow or broaden your inquiry when appropriate, sorting information or items into clear categories

- synthesize multiple sources on the subject to look at information from different points of view, while demonstrating understanding of the subject under investigation

In order to conduct a short or more sustained research project to answer a question or solve a problem, consider the following questions:

- Does my major research question allow me to explore a new issue, an important problem worth solving, or a fresh perspective on a topic?

- Can I research my question within my given time frame and with the resources available to me?

- Have I synthesized multiple sources on the question or problem, looking for different points of view?

- Have I demonstrated understanding of the subject under investigation in my research project?

⟳ YOUR TURN

Read the research questions below. Then, complete the chart by sorting the questions into the correct category. Write the corresponding letter for each question in the appropriate column.

	Research Questions
A	What is Louis Armstrong remembered for?
B	Why did Louis Armstrong specialize in playing the trumpet?
C	How does Nella Larsen's literary work relate to her personal life?
D	What are the events in Nella Larsen's novel *Passing*?
E	How did Louis Armstrong's artistry influence jazz?
F	What was Langston Hughes's poetry about?
G	What beliefs are reflected in Langston Hughes's poetry?
H	Why do people still read Nella Larsen's work today?
I	Who were Langston Hughes's literary inspirations?

Topic	Too Narrow	Appropriate	Too Broad
Louis Armstrong			
Nella Larsen			
Langston Hughes			

YOUR TURN

Develop a research question for formal research. Then, write a short plan of how you will go about doing research for your essay. Include a note about how you might need to modify your plan during the research process.

Process	Plan
Research Question	
Step 1	
Step 2	
Step 3	

Skill:
Evaluating Sources

Once you gather your sources, identify the following:

- where information seems inaccurate, biased, or outdated
- where information strongly relates to your task, purpose, and audience
- where information helps you make an informed decision or solve a problem

In order to conduct advanced searches to gather relevant, credible, and accurate print and digital sources, use the following questions as a guide:

- Is the material published by a well-established source or an expert author?
- Is the source material written by a recognized expert on the topic or a well-respected author or organization?
- Is the material up to date or based on the most current information?
- Is the source based on factual information that can be verified by another source?
- Is the source material objective and unbiased?
- Does the source contain omissions of important information that supports other viewpoints?
- Does the source contain faulty reasoning?
- Are there discrepancies between the information presented in different sources?

In order to refine your search process, consider the following questions:

- Are there specific terms or phrases that I can use to adjust my search?
- Can I use *and, or,* or *not* to expand or limit my search?
- Can I use quotation marks to search for exact phrases?

↻ YOUR TURN

Read the sentences below. Then, complete the chart by sorting the sentences into two categories: those that are credible and reliable and those that are not. Write the corresponding letter for each sentence in the appropriate column.

Sentences	
A	The article states only the author's personal opinions and omits, or leaves out, other positions on the topic.
B	The article includes clear arguments and counterarguments that are supported by factual information.
C	The website is a personal blog or social media website.
D	The author holds a PhD in a discipline related to your topic of research.
E	The text is objective and includes many viewpoints that are properly cited.
F	The text makes unsupported assumptions to persuade readers.

Credible and Reliable	Not Credible or Reliable

⟳ YOUR TURN

Complete the chart below by filling in the title and author of a source for your informative research essay and answering the questions about this source.

Source Questions	Answers
Source Title and Author:	
Reliability: Has the source material been published in a well-established book or periodical or on a well-established website? Is the source material up to date or based on the most current information?	
Accuracy: Is the source based on factual information that can be verified by another source?	
Credibility: Is the source material written by a recognized expert on the topic? Is the source material published by a well-respected author or organization?	
Bias: Is the source material objective and unbiased?	
Omission: Does the source contain omissions of important information that supports other viewpoints?	
Faulty Reasoning: Does the source contain faulty reasoning?	
Decision: Should I use this source in my research report? Is it effective in answering the research question?	

Please note that excerpts and passages in the StudySync® library and this workbook are intended as touchstones to generate interest in an author's work. The excerpts and passages do not substitute for the reading of entire texts, and StudySync® strongly recommends that students seek out and purchase the whole literary or informational work in order to experience it as the author intended. Links to online resellers are available in our digital library. In addition, complete works may be ordered through an authorized reseller by filling out and returning to StudySync® the order form enclosed in this workbook.

Reading & Writing 🖥 **139**
Companion

Skill:
Research and Notetaking

••• CHECKLIST FOR RESEARCH AND NOTETAKING

In order to conduct short as well as more sustained research projects to answer a question (including a self-generated question) or solve a problem, note the following:

- Answer a question for a research project, or think of your own question that you would like to have answered.

- Look up your topic in an encyclopedia to find general information.

- Find specific, up-to-date information in books and periodicals or on the Internet. If appropriate, conduct interviews with experts to get information.

- Narrow or broaden your inquiry when appropriate.

  > If you find dozens of books on a topic, your research topic may be too broad.

  > If it is difficult to write a research question, narrow your topic so it is more specific.

- Synthesize your information by organizing your notes from various sources to see what the sources have in common and how they differ.

To conduct short as well as more sustained research projects to answer a question (including a self-generated question) or solve a problem, consider the following questions:

- Where could I look to find information?

- How does new information I have found affect my research question?

- How can I demonstrate my understanding of the subject I am investigating?

↻ YOUR TURN

Read each point from a student's note cards below. Then, complete the chart by sorting the points into two categories: those that are relevant and those that are not relevant to the writing topic of recorded music during Ma Rainey's time. Write the corresponding letter for each point in the appropriate column.

	Points
A	Source 1: During the Great Migration, music labels sought to make a profit from the highly popular "race music," which was music recorded by African Americans (Timmel).
B	Source 2: According to *History of Minstrelsy,* the purpose of African American minstrel shows differed from those of white performers in that "black minstrel performers felt the added responsibility to counter stereotypes of black identity."
C	Source 3: In 1904, Ma Rainey met and married her husband, William "Pa" Rainey, while performing on tour (Orr).
D	Source 4: The music Rainey recorded with Paramount is of poor quality due to Paramount's "below average recording techniques" (USC Libraries).

Relevant	Not Relevant

Please note that excerpts and passages in the StudySync® library and this workbook are intended as touchstones to generate interest in an author's work. The excerpts and passages do not substitute for the reading of entire texts, and StudySync® strongly recommends that students seek out and purchase the whole literary or informational work in order to experience it as the author intended. Links to online resellers are available in our digital library. In addition, complete works may be ordered through an authorized reseller by filling out and returning to StudySync® the order form enclosed in this workbook.

Reading & Writing Companion 141

YOUR TURN

Complete the chart by synthesizing information from sources relevant to your essay subject's work and personal life. Remember to cite and number each source.

Work	Personal Life

Research Writing Process: Draft

PLAN	DRAFT	REVISE	EDIT AND PUBLISH

You have already made progress toward writing your informative research essay. Now it is time to draft your informative research essay.

✏ WRITE

Use your plan and other responses in your Binder to draft your essay. You may also have new ideas as you begin drafting. Feel free to explore those new ideas as you have them. You can also ask yourself these questions to ensure that your writing is **focused**, **organized**, and **developed**:

Draft Checklist:

☐ **Focused:** Have I made my topic clear to readers? Have I included only relevant information and details and nothing extraneous that might confuse my readers?

☐ **Organized:** Does the organizational structure in my essay make sense? Will readers be engaged by the organization and interested in the way I present information and evidence?

☐ **Developed:** Does my writing include relevant evidence? Will my readers be able to follow my ideas? Will they understand the purpose of my research?

Before you submit your draft, read it over carefully. You want to be sure that you've responded to all aspects of the prompt.

Please note that excerpts and passages in the StudySync® library and this workbook are intended as touchstones to generate interest in an author's work. The excerpts and passages do not substitute for the reading of entire texts, and StudySync® strongly recommends that students seek out and purchase the whole literary or informational work in order to experience it as the author intended. Links to online resellers are available in our digital library. In addition, complete works may be ordered through an authorized reseller by filling out and returning to StudySync® the order form enclosed in this workbook.

Reading & Writing Companion   **143**

Here is Daniela's research essay draft. As you read, notice how Daniela develops her draft to be focused, organized, and developed. As she continues to revise and edit her research essay, she will find and improve weak spots in her writing, as well as correct any language or punctuation mistakes.

 NOTES

STUDENT MODEL: FIRST DRAFT

Post-Reconstruction Blues:

How Gertrude "Ma" Rainey Sang Black Rural Southerners into Popular American Culture

Legendary blues vocalist and Harlem Renaissance artist Gertrude "Ma" Rainey, known as the "Mother of Blues," introduced blues music to a mainstream audience, transforming the genre and expanding opportunities for African American artists. Through depictions of black Southern life and the complex experiences of African American women, Rainey's music increased the visibility of a people silenced in popular culture. While less well-known today, Rainey left a legacy that continues to influence and broaden our knowledge of the Post Reconstruction era.

Ella Pridget gave birth to Ma Rainey, originally Gertrude Malissa Nix Pridgett, on April 26, 1886, in Columbus, Georgia. Rainey posessed a musical talent from a young age and performed in public for the first time at age 14 at the Springer Opera House in Columbus. Soon after, she found her calling singing on tour in vaudeville and African American minstral shows. For more than thirty years, performed in troupes, such as F.S. Wolcott's Rabbit Foot Minstrels and Tolliver's Circus and Musical Extravaganza.

~~Ma Rainey used vaudeville and minstrel shows as a platform to showcase her talent. She also used them to share her life experiences. Vaudeville originated from minstrel shows. It became popular at the turn of the century. Vaudeville shows featured unrelated acts such as singing, dancing, comedy, acrobatics, and magic. While no video recordings of Ma Rainey exist, the memory of her vibrint performances have been passed down through written reviews. According to critic Mary L. Bogumil in *Understanding August Wilson*, Rainey wore "flamboyant" jewelry and costmes and performed in front of a~~

~~backdrop that featured a large gramophone designe, "which gave the appearance of Ma emerging right from the speaker, issuing from and manifesting the music itself" (Timmel). Such extravagant details show the sensational nature of vaudeville shows. Rainey's bold and brilliant stage persona was magnetic she forced the audience, who were often men, to listen to what she had to say.~~

Vaudeville: Ma Rainey's Early Career

Ma Rainey used vaudeville and minstrel shows as a platform to showcase her talent and share her life experiences. Originating from minstrel shows, vaudeville became popular at the turn of the century and featured unrelated acts such as singing, dancing, comedy, acrobatics, and magic. While no video recordings of Ma Rainey exist, the memory of her vibrant performances has been passed down through written reviews. According to critic Mary L. Bogumil in *Understanding August Wilson*, Rainey wore "flamboyant" jewelry and costumes and performed in front of a backdrop that featured a large gramophone design, "which gave the appearance of Ma emerging right from the speaker, issuing from and manifesting the music itself" (qtd. in Timmel). Such extravagant details exemplify the sensational nature of vaudeville shows. Rainey's bold and brilliant stage persona was magnetic. She forced the audience, who were often men, to listen to what she had to say.

~~The variety show format of vaudeville allowed performers to communicate larger themes to the audience. For example, PBS's American Masters says of immigrant performers, "Their acts were a form of assimilation, in which they could become active parts of popular culture through representations of their heritage" ("Vaudeville: About Vaudeville"). However, as an African American woman, she belonged to a class of citizens who were underrepresented, misunderstood, and discriminated against. Ma Rainey was not an immigrant. Like the immigrants, she used the modes of performance available to her to cross racial and class boundaries and bring the experiences of a Southern African American women into the main stream ("Vaudeville: About Vaudeville").~~

Skill: Print and Graphic Features

Daniela decides that while her body paragraphs flow together, she could make her points clearer by using headings. So she inserts a heading between her second and third paragraphs. As she continues to reread her essay, she will add a heading wherever she discusses a new aspect of Ma Rainey's work and life.

Skill: Paraphrasing

Daniela realizes she has taken the phrase "to cross racial and class boundaries" word-for-word from her source. To avoid plagiarism, she can either paraphrase the information or quote it. Since she already has one quotation from this source in the paragraph, she decides to paraphrase.

Skill:
Critiquing Research

Daniela notices that instead of synthesizing information from several sources, she has used only one source in the paragraph. To round out her explanation of vaudeville and Ma Rainey's role in it, she integrates another idea from a different source into the paragraph.

The variety show format of vaudeville allowed performers to communicate larger themes to the audience. For example, PBS's *American Masters* says of immigrant performers, "Their acts were a form of assimilation, in which they could become active parts of popular culture through representations of their heritage" ("Vaudeville: About Vaudeville"). In other words, immigrant performers used the highly adaptable and entertaining structure of vaudeville to disseminate information about where they came from. Ma Rainey was not an immigrant. However, as an African American woman, she belonged to a class of citizens who were underrepresented, misunderstood, and discriminated against. Like the immigrants, she used the modes of performance available to her to subvert boundaries and bring the experiences of a Southern African American women into the mainstream ("Vaudeville: About Vaudeville"). That Ma Rainey was also the first woman to include blues music in her act only further illustrates her ability to use this mode of performance to break barriers and convey an important message (Orr).

The blues played a central part in Rainey's performances. Originating in the South at the turn of the century, blues came from such African musical traditions as field hollers, work songs, spirituals, and country string ballads ("What Is the Blues?"). Most blues songs follow a 12 bar structure with an AAB verse pattern where "the first and second lines are repeated, and the third line is a response to them—often with a twist" ("Understanding the 12-Bar Blues"). Blues music tends to explore melancholy topics, such as sadness, desire, and longing. Many of Rainey's songs had a melancholy tone, her music served to empower women by approaching topics most women could not discuss freely. For example, Ma Rainey's candid discussion of love was unique to blues artists of her time. She was lonely but also embraced her independence ("I don't want no man to put sugar in my tea."). Rainey's rejection of a male partner was radical because women in this time period were expected to build their lives around being married and building a family. In *Blues Legacies and Black Feminism*, Angela Davis points out that "black women of that era were acknowledging and addressing issues central to contemporary feminist discourse" (Davis 28). Black female blues artists like Ma

Rainey were ahead of their time in terms of asserting their agency. Rainey's performance of this song introduced the idea of liberated black women into the mainstream.

~~Rainey's vocals had a deep and unbellished tone expressing raw emotion that resonated with a wide range of audiences. The gravelly timbre of her . . . raspy, deep voice (Orr) as well as her "moaning style" entranced listeners. Her flashy visual representation attracted the attention of the audience. Her measured and gripping delivery kept them waiting for more. Ma Rainey one of the first professional female blues artists to make a phonograph record. During the Great Migration, blues music spread from the South into other regions of the nation. By the 1920s, recording labels saw a market for "race records," or music created by and for African Americans. After establishing her career as a touring musician, Ma Rainey recorded over 100 songs with Paramount in the span of 1923 to 1928. One could argue that Paramount exploited Ma Rainey for corporate gane. However, in 1928 Paramount stopped recording with Rainey after determining that race records like hers were no longer profitable. Still, making a phonograph record with Paramount did help Rainey's audience and success grow. Over the course of her career, she performed alongside various bands and other renowned Harlem Renaissance muzicians, such as Louis Armstrong and Bessie Smith.~~

Rainey's vocals had a deep and unembellished tone expressing raw emotion that resonated with a wide range of audiences. "The gravelly timbre of her . . . raspy, deep voice" (Orr) as well as her "moaning style" (Timmel) entranced listeners. Her flashy visual representation attracted the attention of the audience. Her measured and gripping delivery kept them waiting for more. Ma Rainey was one of the first professional female blues artists to make a phonograph record. During the Great Migration, blues music spread from the South into other regions of the nation. [Include graphic] By the 1920s, recording labels saw a market for "race records," or music created by and for African Americans. After establishing her career as a touring musician, Ma Rainey

Skill: Sources and Citations

Daniela forgot to add quotation marks around the description from N. Lee Orr, so she adds them. In the same sentence, she forgot to add a parenthetical citation for the quotation "moaning style." She includes the author's name in the citation, but since the source is electronic, she doesn't add a page number.

NOTES

recorded over 100 songs with Paramount in the span of 1923 to 1928 (Timmel). However, in 1928 Paramount stopped recording with Rainey after determining that race records like hers were no longer profitable. One could argue that Paramount exploited Ma Rainey for corporate gain. Still, making a phonograph record with Paramount did help Rainey's audience and success grow. Over the course of her career, she performed alongside various bands and other renowned Harlem Renaissance musicians, such as Louis Armstrong and Bessie Smith.

In an era when women of color had limited possibilities, "The Mother of Blues," Ma Rainey, was a musician who took advantage of the modes of performance that were available to her to build a long lasting career. Rainey used the public platforms of vaudeville and recorded music. Her lyrics talked about her experiences and feelings. Ma Rainey's unique style appealed to many people, helping bring the blues and her life experiences to a mainstream audience.

Works Cited

Biography.com Editors. "Ma Rainey Biography." *The Biography.com Website,* A&E Television Networks, Published 2 Apr. 2014, Updated 27 Apr. 2017, https://www.biography.com/people/ma-rainey-9542413. Accessed 20 Sep. 2018.

Davis, Angela Y. Blues Legacies and Black Feminism: Gertrude "Ma" Rainey, Bessie Smith, and Billie Holiday. *Google Books.* 2nd ed., Vintage Books, 1999.

Orr, N. Lee. "Gertrude 'Ma' Rainey (1886-1939)." *New Georgia Encyclopedia,* Georgia State University, 9 May 2003, https://www.georgiaencyclopedia.org/articles/arts-culture/gertrude-ma-rainey-1886–1939. Accessed 20 Sep. 2018.

Timmel, Lisa. "The Music of Ma Rainey." *Huntington Theater Company*, Accessed 20 Sep. 2018.

"Understanding the 12-Bar Blues." *PBS: The Blues,* 2003, www.pbs.org/theblues/classroom/essays12bar.html. Accessed 21 Sep. 2018.

"Vaudeville: About Vaudeville." *PBS: American Masters,* 8 Oct. 1999, www.pbs.org/wnet/americanmasters/vaudeville-about-vaudeville/721/. Accessed 20 Sep. 2018.

"What Is the Blues?" *PBS: The Blues,* 2003, www.pbs.org/theblues/classroom/essaysblues.html. Accessed 21 Sep. 2018.

Please note that excerpts and passages in the StudySync® library and this workbook are intended as touchstones to generate interest in an author's work. The excerpts and passages do not substitute for the reading of entire texts, and StudySync® strongly recommends that students seek out and purchase the whole literary or informational work in order to experience it as the author intended. Links to online resellers are available in our digital library. In addition, complete works may be ordered through an authorized reseller by filling out and returning to StudySync® the order form enclosed in this workbook.

Reading & Writing Companion

149

Skill:
Critiquing Research

••• CHECKLIST FOR CRITIQUING RESEARCH

In order to conduct short or sustained research projects to answer a question or solve a problem, drawing on several sources, do the following:

- narrow or broaden the question or inquiry as necessary when researching your topic

- use advanced search terms effectively when looking for information online, such as using unique terms that are specific to your topic (i.e., "daily life in Jamestown, Virginia" rather than just "Jamestown, Virginia")

- assess the strengths and limitations of each source in terms of the task, purpose, and audience

- synthesize and integrate multiple sources on a subject

To evaluate and use relevant information while conducting short or sustained research projects, consider the following questions:

- Did I narrow or broaden my research inquiry as needed?

- Are there specific terms or phrases in my research question that I can use to adjust my search?

- Can I use *and, or,* or *not* to expand or limit my search?

- Can I use quotation marks to search for exact phrases?

- Have I successfully synthesized and integrated multiple sources on my topic?

⟳ YOUR TURN

Read the previous draft of Daniela's research plan. Then, answer the multiple-choice questions.

> Major Research Question: Did Ma Rainey influence other musicians?
>
> List of Sources:
> 1. Facebook Post: Bessie Smith v. Ma Rainey
> 2. The Legacy of Blues Musicians: Mamie Smith, Ma Rainey, and Beyond (television documentary)
> 3. Britannica.com: Ma Rainey's Blues Style
> 4. Classic Blues Magazine: Classic Blues Traditions, Then and Now

1. Which revision of her major research question will best refocus her research plan?

   ○ A. What are the topics of Ma Rainey's lyrics?
   ○ B. How did Ma Rainey's blues style influence other musicians?
   ○ C. Why was Bessie Smith a successful blues singer?
   ○ D. The research question is already focused.

2. Which source should Daniela consider replacing?

   ○ A. 1
   ○ B. 2
   ○ C. 3
   ○ D. 4

✎ WRITE

Write your major research question, and list your sources. Then, use the questions in the checklist to critique your research plan. In your critique, evaluate the appropriateness of your sources and determine whether your research plan needs a revision.

Please note that excerpts and passages in the StudySync® library and this workbook are intended as touchstones to generate interest in an author's work. The excerpts and passages do not substitute for the reading of entire texts, and StudySync® strongly recommends that students seek out and purchase the whole literary or informational work in order to experience it as the author intended. Links to online resellers are available in our digital library. In addition, complete works may be ordered through an authorized reseller by filling out and returning to StudySync® the order form enclosed in this workbook.

Reading & Writing **151**
Companion

Skill:
Paraphrasing

In order to integrate information into your research essay, first make sure you understand what the author is saying after reading the text carefully. Then, note the following:

- any words or expressions that are unfamiliar

- words and phrases that are important to include in a paraphrase to maintain the meaning of the text

- potential instances of plagiarism; avoid plagiarism by acknowledging all sources for both paraphrased and quoted material, and avoid overly relying on any one source

- whether or not your integration of information maintains a logical flow of ideas

To integrate information into your research essay, consider the following questions:

- Do I understand the meaning of the text?

- Have I determined the meanings of any words in the text that are unfamiliar to me?

- Does my paraphrase of the text maintain the text's original meaning? Have I missed any key points or details?

- Have I avoided plagiarism by acknowledging all my sources for both paraphrased and quoted material and avoided overly relying on any one source?

- Did I integrate information selectively to maintain a logical flow of ideas?

↻ YOUR TURN

Choose the best answer to each question.

1. The following is a quotation that Daniela is considering including in her essay. Which of the following sentences provides the best paraphrase of the source text?

> "Today, the blues no longer commands the attention it once did; to many young listeners, traditional blues—if not contemporary blues—may sound antiquated and uninteresting."

- ○ A. Once a very popular genre, blues music is not as widely enjoyed by today's young listeners.
- ○ B. Many young listeners are unfamiliar with the blues today.
- ○ C. The history of traditional blues spans several generations.
- ○ D. Today, the blues no longer commands the attention it once did.

2. The following is a paragraph from a previous draft of Daniela's essay. How could paraphrasing best help Daniela improve this paragraph?

> Rainey's vocals had a deep and unembellished tone expressing raw emotion that resonated with a wide range of audiences. "The gravelly timbre of her . . . raspy, deep voice" (Orr) as well as her "moaning style" (Timmel) entranced listeners. "Her material consisted of a variety of songs drawn from Southern traditions" (Timmel) and her flashy visual representation attracted the attention of the audience. Her measured and gripping delivery kept them waiting for more. Ma Rainey was one of the first professional female blues artists to make a phonograph record. During the Great Migration, blues music spread from the South into other regions of the nation. By the 1920s, recording labels saw a market for "race records," (Timmel) or music created by and for African Americans. After establishing her career as a touring musician, Ma Rainey "laid down over 100 tracks between 1923 and 1928" (Timmel).

- ○ A. Paraphrasing would help improve this paragraph by showing that Daniela thoroughly read each of her sources.
- ○ B. Paraphrasing would improve her paragraph by making it shorter and quicker to read.
- ○ C. Paraphrasing would increase Daniela's chances of plagiarizing information.
- ○ D. Paraphrasing would help improve her paragraph by avoiding so many back-to-back quotations and maintaining a logical flow of ideas.

✐ WRITE

Use the questions in the checklist to paraphrase information from a source and integrate it into a paragraph of your informative research essay.

Skill:
Sources and Citations

••• CHECKLIST FOR SOURCES AND CITATIONS

In order to gather relevant information from multiple authoritative print and digital sources and to cite the sources correctly, do the following:

- gather information from a variety of print and digital sources, using search terms to effectively narrow your search

- assess the strengths and limitations of each source in regard to your task, your purpose for writing, and your audience

  > find information on authors to see if they are experts on a topic

  > look at the publication date to see if the information is current

  > avoid relying on any one source, and synthesize information from a variety of books, publications, and online resources

  > quote or paraphrase the information you find, and cite it to avoid plagiarism

  > integrate information selectively to maintain a logical flow of ideas in your essay, using transitional words and phrases

- include all sources in a bibliography, following a standard format:

  > Halall, Ahmed. *The Pyramids of Ancient Egypt*. New York: Central Publishing, 2016.

  > for a citation, footnote, or endnote, include the author, title, and page number

To check that you have gathered information and cited sources correctly, consider the following questions:

- Have I assessed the strengths and limitations of each source?

- Have I looked for different points of view, instead of relying on one source?

- Did I cite the information I found using a standard format to avoid plagiarism?

- Did I include all my sources in my bibliography?

⟳ YOUR TURN

Choose the best answer to each question.

1. Below is a section from a previous draft of Daniela's research paper. What change should Daniela make to improve the clarity of her citation?

> Author Sandra R. Lieb writes, "The Classic Blues barely outlived the twenties, becoming engulfed in and utterly changed by the Depression and shifts in audience taste, but from 1920 to roughly 1928 Ma Rainey and [other women singers] were the greatest artists, enjoying a period of influence, wealth, popularity, and imitation by lesser performers."

- ○ A. Add the page number in parentheses after the quotation.
- ○ B. Add the author's last name in parentheses after the quotation.
- ○ C. Add the author's last name and page number in parentheses after the quotation.
- ○ D. No change needs to be made.

2. Below is a section from a previous draft of Daniela's works cited page in the MLA format. Which revision best corrects her style errors?

> *Mother of Blues: A Study of Ma Rainey.* by Sandra R. Lieb. University of Massachusetts Press, 1981.

- ○ A. Lieb, Sandra R. Mother of Blues: A Study of Ma Rainey. University of Massachusetts Press, 1981.
- ○ B. University of Massachusetts Press, 1981. Lieb, Sandra R. *Mother of Blues: A Study of Ma Rainey*.
- ○ C. Lieb, Sandra R. *Mother of Blues: A Study of Ma Rainey*. University of Massachusetts Press.
- ○ D. Lieb, Sandra R. *Mother of Blues: A Study of Ma Rainey*. University of Massachusetts Press, 1981.

✎ WRITE

Use the questions in the checklist to revise your in-text citations and works cited list.

Check that your information, whether quoted or paraphrased, is properly cited to avoid plagiarism. Refer to the *MLA Handbook* as needed.

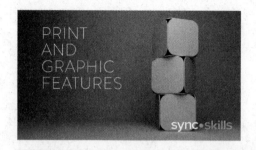

Skill:
Print and Graphic Features

••• CHECKLIST FOR PRINT AND GRAPHIC FEATURES

In order to check your draft for the inclusion of print and graphic features, first reread your draft and ask yourself the following questions:

- To what extent would including formatting, graphics, or multimedia be effective in achieving my purpose?
- Which formatting, graphics, or multimedia seem most important in conveying information to the reader?
- How is the addition of the formatting, graphics, or multimedia useful in aiding comprehension?

To include formatting, graphics, and multimedia, use the following questions as a guide:

- How can I use formatting to better organize information? Consider adding:

  > titles
  > headings
  > subheadings
  > bullets
  > boldface and italicized terms

- How can I use graphics to better convey information? Consider adding:

  > charts
  > graphs
  > tables
  > timelines
  > diagrams
  > maps
  > figures and statistics

- How can I use multimedia to add interest and variety? Consider adding a combination of:

  > photographs
  > art
  > audio
  > video

 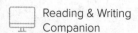

⟳ YOUR TURN

Choose the best answer to each question.

1. Read the following two paragraphs from another draft of Daniela's essay. Then, decide which of the possible headings below would best improve the flow of information between the two paragraphs.

> The variety show format of vaudeville allowed performers to communicate larger themes to the audience. For example, PBS's *American Masters* says of immigrant performers, "Their acts were a form of assimilation, in which they could become active parts of popular culture through representations of their heritage" ("Vaudeville: About Vaudeville"). In other words, immigrant performers used the highly adaptable and entertaining structure of vaudeville to disseminate information about where they came from. Ma Rainey was not an immigrant. However, as an African American woman, she belonged to a class of citizens who were underrepresented, misunderstood, and discriminated against. Like the immigrants, she used the modes of performance available to her "to cross racial and class boundaries" ("Vaudeville: About Vaudeville") and bring the experiences of a Southern African American women into the mainstream.
>
> The blues played a central part in Rainey's performances. Originating in the South at the turn of the century, blues emerged from such African musical traditions as field hollers, work songs, spirituals, and country string ballads ("What Is the Blues?"). Most blues songs follow a 12-bar structure with an AAB verse pattern where "the first and second lines are repeated, and the third line is a response to them—often with a twist" ("Understanding the 12-Bar Blues"). Blues music tends to explore melancholy topics, such as sadness, desire, and longing. While many of Rainey's songs had a melancholy tone, her music also served to empower women by approaching topics most women could not discuss freely.

○ A. "Moving On From Vaudeville"
○ B. "Ma Rainey and Her Influence on the Blues"
○ C. "The Blues"
○ D. Daniela does not need to include a heading between these two paragraphs.

✎ WRITE

Use the questions in the checklist to review your informative research essay and locate where you can place headings to call out specific sections and topics. Then, note areas where you would like to add graphics or media, and describe what sort of features you might include and why.

Research Writing Process: Revise

PLAN	DRAFT	REVISE	EDIT AND PUBLISH

You have written a draft of your informative research essay. You have also received input from your peers about how to improve it. Now you are going to revise your draft.

 ## REVISION GUIDE

Examine your draft to find areas for revision. Use the guide below to help you review:

Review	Revise	Example
Clarity		
Highlight a sentence that shows your purpose for writing.	Make sure the purpose is specific and clearly stated for your audience.	While less well-known today, Rainey left a legacy that continues to influence musicians and broaden our knowledge of life for African Americans in the Post-Reconstruction era.
Development		
Identify the textual evidence you quote in support of your thesis.	Rather than letting quotations speak for themselves, make sure you provide original commentary to build upon your evidence from sources.	For example, PBS's *American Masters* says of immigrant performers, "Their acts were a form of assimilation, in which they could become active parts of popular culture through representations of their heritage" ("Vaudeville: About Vaudeville"). In other words, immigrant performers used the highly adaptable and entertaining structure of vaudeville to disseminate information about where they came from.

Review	Revise	Example
Organization		
Review your body paragraphs. Are they focused and logically organized? Identify and annotate any sentences within and across paragraphs that don't flow in a clear and logical way.	Rewrite the sentences so they appear in a clear and logical order.	One could argue that Paramount exploited Ma Rainey for corporate gane. However, in 1928 Paramount stopped recording with Rainey after determining that race records like hers were no longer profitable. ~~One could argue that Paramount exploited Ma Rainey for corporate gane.~~ Still, making a phonograph record with Paramount did help Rainey's audience and success grow.
Style: Word Choice		
Identify any weak adjectives or verbs.	Replace weak adjectives and verbs with strong, descriptive adjectives and verbs.	Such extravagant details ~~show~~ exemplify the sensational nature of vaudeville shows.
Style: Sentence Fluency		
Read aloud your writing and listen to the way the text sounds. Does it sound choppy? Or does it flow smoothly with rhythm, movement, and emphasis on important details and events?	Rewrite a key passage, making your sentences longer or shorter to achieve a better flow of writing.	Ma Rainey used vaudeville and minstrel shows as a platform to showcase her talent. ~~She also used them to~~ and share her life experiences. ~~Vaudeville originated~~ Originating from minstrel shows~~,~~. ~~It~~ vaudeville became popular at the turn of the century. ~~Vaudeville shows~~ and featured unrelated acts such as singing, dancing, comedy, acrobatics, and magic.

✏ WRITE

Use the revision guide, as well as your peer reviews, to help you evaluate your informative research essay to determine places that should be revised.

Skill:
Using a Style Guide

Copyright © BookheadEd Learning, LLC

••• CHECKLIST FOR USING A STYLE GUIDE

In order to write your work so that it conforms to the guidelines in a style manual, do the following:

- Determine which style guide you should use before you write your draft.

  > Follow the guidelines chosen by a teacher, for example.

  > Familiarize yourself with that guide, and check your writing against the guide when you edit.

- Use the style guide for the overall formatting of your paper, citation style, bibliography format, and other style considerations for reporting research.

As you draft, use an additional style guide, such as *Artful Sentences: Syntax as Style* by Virginia Tufte, to help you vary your syntax, or the grammatical structure of sentences.

  > Use a variety of simple, compound, complex, and compound-complex sentences to convey information.

  > Be sure to punctuate your sentences correctly.

  > Follow standard English language conventions to help you maintain a formal style for formal papers.

To edit your work so that it conforms to the guidelines in a style manual, consider the following questions:

- Have I followed the conventions for spelling, punctuation, capitalization, sentence structure, and formatting, according to the style guide?

- Have I varied my syntax to make my information clear for readers?

- Do I have an entry in my works cited or bibliography for each reference I used?

- Have I followed the correct style, including the guidelines for capitalization and punctuation, in each entry in my works cited or bibliography?

YOUR TURN

Read the types of information below. Then, complete the chart by sorting them into two categories: those that are found in a style guide and those that are not. Write the corresponding letter for each type of information in the appropriate column.

Types of Information	
A. proper punctuation for quotations	**F.** a list of possible research topics
B. synonyms for a word	**G.** how to format a bibliography
C. how to read a map	**H.** how to cite Internet sources
D. when to use a hyphen	**I.** the definition of a word
E. how to write an outline	**J.** when to use italics

In a Style Guide	Not in a Style Guide

✏ **WRITE**

Use the checklist to help you choose a convention that you have found challenging to follow. Use a credible style guide to check and correct any errors related to that convention in your informative research essay.

Grammar:
Contested Usage

For most formal writing, it is probably advisable to follow the traditional rules of grammar. In most cases, following the rules will improve both the clarity and effectiveness of your communication. However, there are a number of grammar "rules" that can be broken if you have a good reason to do so. The most important thing to keep in mind is that no rule of grammar should be broken unless it is done deliberately to improve the effectiveness of your writing.

The series comma is still widely used and preferred for a series of three or more items. However, in recent years, its necessity has come into question. Many authors of formal and informal writing find that they can use other strategies that eliminate the need for the series comma.

Strategy	Text
Sometimes you can omit a series comma if the wording clearly indicates a new phrase in the series.	Paul writes novels, paints pottery and designs gardens.
Sometimes you can omit a series comma if single words are clearly related to one reference or topic.	In an attempt to get to the bottom of the question once and for all, the *Guardian* has gathered writers from the fields of science, psychotherapy, literature, religion and philosophy to give their definition of the much-pondered word. What is Love?

The words *whom* and *who* are a great example of contested diction. *Who* is a subject pronoun, like *he, she,* or *they*. It is used as a subject in a main clause that asks a question or as the subject in a subordinate clause. *Whom* is an object pronoun, like *him, her,* or *them*. It is used in place of *who* as the direct object that receives the action of a verb or as the object of a preposition. If you are writing for an informational or research purpose, use *whom* when referring to a pronoun as an object. However, if you are writing informally, with contemporary dialogue, colloquialisms, or slang, it is appropriate to eliminate the use of *whom*.

Occasionally, writers choose to begin sentences with coordinating conjunctions. Writers use coordinating conjunctions as sentence openers when they want to indicate a relationship with the previous sentence but do not want to combine the two complete thoughts into one sentence. This is usually done to emphasize the second of two related ideas.

Strategy	Text
If you are writing two or three sentences that are closely related and have equal importance, you could use a coordinating conjunction such as *and* or *but* as a sentence opener.	So when Miss Lawington told me about the cakes I thought that I could bake them and earn enough at one time to increase the net value of the flock the equivalent of two head. And that by saving the eggs out one at a time, even the eggs wouldn't be costing anything.
	As I Lay Dying

⟳ YOUR TURN

1. When can a series comma be omitted?

   ○ A. A series comma must always be used, even if the objects are clearly related to one reference or topic.

   ○ B. A series comma can be omitted if single items are clearly related to one reference or topic.

2. Is the removal of the series comma in this sentence acceptable?

   > Would you like your eggs scrambled, fried or poached?

   ○ A. Yes, removing the series comma is acceptable.

   ○ B. No, removing the series comma is unacceptable.

3. Is this use of a coordinating conjunction as a sentence opener acceptable?

   > He spent his vacation in Naples, Florida. But he said it was a business trip, not a pleasure trip.

   ○ A. Yes, it is an acceptable use of a coordinating conjunction as a sentence opener.

   ○ B. No, it is an unacceptable use of a coordinating conjunction as a sentence opener.

4. Is this an acceptable use of *who*?

   > In 1864, Twain, who fortune still eluded, went to San Francisco where he worked on several newspapers.

   ○ A. Yes, it is an acceptable use of *who*.

   ○ B. No, it is an unacceptable use of *who*. It should be replaced with *whom*.

Grammar: Hyphens

Hyphens join words or parts of words. Do not use any type of dash where a hyphen is needed.

Rule	Text	Explanation
Use a hyphen after any prefix joined to a proper noun or a proper adjective, for example, *pre-Depression*. Use a hyphen after the prefixes *all-, ex-* (meaning "former"), and *self-* joined to any noun or adjective. Use a hyphen after the prefix *anti-* when it is joined to a word beginning with *i*. Also, use a hyphen after the prefix *vice-*, except in *vice president*.	Every Tory is a coward; for servile, slavish, **self-interested** fear is the foundation of Toryism; and a man under such influence, though he may be cruel, never can be brave. The Crisis	The prefix **self-** is joined to the word **interested** with a hyphen.
Hyphenate any compound word that is a spelled-out cardinal number (such as *twenty-one*) or ordinal number (such as *twenty-first*) up to *ninety-nine* or *ninety-ninth*. Hyphenate any spelled-out fraction.	**One-eighth** of the whole population were . . . slaves, not distributed generally over the Union, but localized in the southern part of it. Lincoln's Second Inaugural Address	**One-eighth** is a fraction.
Use a hyphen in a compound adjective that precedes a noun. Be sure to choose words carefully as the words should work together to provide a unified meaning.	It might be, too, that a witch, like old Mistress Hibbins, the **bitter-tempered** widow of the magistrate, was to die upon the gallows. The Scarlet Letter	The words **bitter-tempered** are hyphenated as a compound adjective that modifies the noun *widow*.

⟳ YOUR TURN

1. How should this sentence be changed?

> Sandra Wilson—the exmayor of our fair city—spoke warmly of the new, experienced mayor.

- ○ A. Change **exmayor** to **ex-mayor.**
- ○ B. Change the dashes to hyphens.
- ○ C. Change **new, experienced** to **new-experienced.**
- ○ D. No change needs to be made to this sentence.

2. How should this sentence be changed?

> The short-tempered coach made the team do twenty five extra sit-ups before the end of practice—how unfair!

- ○ A. Remove the hyphen in **short-tempered.**
- ○ B. Change **twenty five** to **twenty-five.**
- ○ C. Change the dash to a hyphen.
- ○ D. No change needs to be made to this sentence.

3. How should this sentence be changed?

> My grandfather—a two-tour veteran—loves telling stories about how newfound optimism spread through post–World War II America.

- ○ A. Change the dashes to hyphens.
- ○ B. Change **newfound** to **new-found.**
- ○ C. Change **post–World War II** to **post World War II.**
- ○ D. No change needs to be made to this sentence.

Please note that excerpts and passages in the StudySync® library and this workbook are intended as touchstones to generate interest in an author's work. The excerpts and passages do not substitute for the reading of entire texts, and StudySync® strongly recommends that students seek out and purchase the whole literary or informational work in order to experience it as the author intended. Links to online resellers are available in our digital library. In addition, complete works may be ordered through an authorized reseller by filling out and returning to StudySync® the order form enclosed in this workbook.

Reading & Writing
Companion

165

Research Writing Process: Edit and Publish

PLAN	DRAFT	REVISE	EDIT AND PUBLISH

You have revised your informative research essay based on your peer feedback and your own examination.

Now, it is time to edit your essay. When you revised, you focused on the content of your essay. You probably critiqued your research and made sure you paraphrased sources correctly and avoided plagiarism. When you edit, you focus on the mechanics of your writing, paying close attention to things like grammar and punctuation.

Use the checklist below to guide you as you edit:

☐ Have I followed all the rules for hyphens?

☐ Have I checked for contested usage and selected the usage that is most appropriate for my purpose?

☐ Do I have any sentence fragments or run-on sentences?

☐ Have I spelled everything correctly?

Notice some edits Daniela has made:

- Used the passive voice to remove less important information

- Corrected spelling errors

- Added a subject to correct a sentence fragment

~~Ella Pridget gave birth to Ma Rainey, originally~~ Ma Rainey was born Gertrude Malissa Nix Pridgett~~,~~ on April 26, 1886, in Columbus, Georgia. Rainey ~~posessed~~ possessed a musical talent from a young age and performed in public for the first time at age 14 at the Springer Opera House in Columbus. Soon after, she found her calling singing on tour in vaudeville and African American ~~minstral~~ minstrel shows. For more than thirty years, Rainey performed in troupes, such as F.S. Wolcott's Rabbit Foot Minstrels and Tolliver's Circus and Musical Extravaganza.

✏ WRITE

Use the questions in the checklist, as well as your peer reviews, to help you evaluate your informative research essay to determine areas that need editing. Then, edit your essay to correct those errors.

Once you have made all your corrections, you are ready to publish your work. You can distribute your writing to family and friends, hang it on a bulletin board, or post it on your blog. If you publish online, share the link with your family, friends, and classmates.

Please note that excerpts and passages in the StudySync® library and this workbook are intended as touchstones to generate interest in an author's work. The excerpts and passages do not substitute for the reading of entire texts, and StudySync® strongly recommends that students seek out and purchase the whole literary or informational work in order to experience it as the author intended. Links to online resellers are available in our digital library. In addition, complete works may be ordered through an authorized reseller by filling out and returning to StudySync® the order form enclosed in this workbook.

Reading & Writing Companion   **167**

PHOTO/IMAGE CREDITS:

cover, iStock.com/Alex Potemkin
p. iii, iStock.com/DNY59
p. ix, iStock.com/Alex Potemkin
p. x, Chimamanda Ngozi Adichie - Taylor Hill/
Contributor/FilmMagic/Getty Images
p. x, John F. Carter, Jr - Public Domain
p. x, Kate Chopin - Public Domain
p. x, Paul Laurence Dunbar - Anthony Barboza/
Contributor/Archive Photos/Getty Images
p. x, Alice Dunbar Nelson - Interim Archives/
Contributor/Archive Photos/Getty Images
p. x, Ralph Waldo Ellison - Everett Collection
Historical/Alamy Stock Photo
p. xi, William Faulkner - Eric Schaal/Contributor/The
LIFE Images Collection/Getty Images
p. xi, F. Scott Fitzgerald - American Stock Archive/
Contributor/Archive Photos/Getty Images
p. xi, Charlotte Perkins Gilman - Public Domain
p. xi, Ernest Hemingway - World History Archive/
Alamy Stock Photo
p. xi, Langston Hughes - Underwood Archives/
Contributor/Archive Photos/Getty Images
p. xii, iStock.com/LordRunar
p. 1, Topical Press Agency/Hulton Archive/Getty
Images
p. 2, Bettmann/Bettmann/Getty Images
p. 5, iStock.com/LordRunar
p. 6, LoraLiu/iStock.com
p. 7, Fotosearch/Archive Photos/Getty Images
p. 25, LoraLiu/iStock.com
p. 26, iStock.com/Orla
p. 27, iStock.com/Orla
p. 28, LoraLiu/iStock.com
p. 29, iStock.com/Blackbeck
p. 30, Public Domain Image
p. 33, iStock.com/Blackbeck
p. 34, iStock.com/urbancow
p. 35, iStock.com/urbancow
p. 36, iStock.com/LdF
p. 37, iStock.com/LdF
p. 38, iStock.com/Blackbeck
p. 39, iStock.com/Yuri_Arcurs
p. 43, Mondadori Portfolio/Mondadori Portfolio/Getty
Images
p. 46, iStock.com/cristianl
p. 51, iStock.com/cristianl
p. 52, iStock.com/LdF
p. 53, iStock.com/LdF
p. 54, iStock.com/cristianl
p. 55, iStock.com/wragg
p. 60, iStock.com/SondraP
p. 70, iStock.com/Boogich

p. 72, Anthony Barboza/Archive Photos/Getty
Images
p. 74, Library of Congress/Corbis Historical/Getty
Images
p. 77, iStock.com/Boogich
p. 78, Alfred Eisenstaedt/Contributor/The LIFE
Picture Collection/Getty Images
p. 79, Alfred Eisenstaedt/Contributor/The LIFE
Picture Collection/Getty Images
p. 81, Peter Horree/Alamy Stock Photo
p. 83, Alfred Eisenstaedt/Contributor/The LIFE
Picture Collection/Getty Images
p. 84, iStock.com/S. Greg Panosian
p. 92, ©iStock.com/DanBrandenburg
p. 93, Public Domain Image
p. 94, Public Domain Image
p. 95, Public Domain Image
p. 96, iStock.com/Gregory_DUBUS
p. 97, Hulton Archive/Archive Photos/Getty Images
p. 99, istock.com/LeoPatrizi
p. 103, iStock.com/margotpics
p. 108, iStock.com/margotpics
p. 109, iStock.com/ThomasVogel
p. 110, iStock.com/ThomasVogel
p. 111, iStock.com/fotogaby
p. 112, iStock.com/fotogaby
p. 113, iStock.com/Brostock
p. 114, iStock.com/Brostock
p. 115, iStock.com/margotpics
p. 116, iStock.com/Peeter Viisimaa
p. 120, iStock.com/Peeter Viisimaa
p. 121, iStock.com/urbancow
p. 122, iStock.com/urbancow
p. 123, iStock.com/Peeter Viisimaa
p. 124, iStock.com/hanibaram, iStock.com/seb_ra,
iStock.com/Martin Barraud
p. 125, iStock.com/Martin Barraud
p. 129, Michael Ochs Archives/Michael Ochs
Archives/Getty Images
p. 130, StudySync Graphic
p. 134, iStock.com/koya79
p. 137, iStock.com/Mutlu Kurtbas
p. 140, iStock.com/DNY59
p. 143, iStock.com/Martin Barraud
p. 150, iStock.com/SKrow
p. 152, iStock.com/horiyan
p. 154, iStock.com/tofumax
p. 156, iStock.com/me4o
p. 158, iStock.com/Martin Barraud
p. 160, iStock.com/Customdesigner
p. 162, ©iStock.com/wingmar
p. 164, ©iStock.com/Thomas Shanahan
p. 166, iStock.com/Martin Barraud

studysync®

Text Fulfillment Through StudySync

If you are interested in specific titles, please fill out the form below and we will check availability through our partners.

ORDER DETAILS

Date:

TITLE	AUTHOR	Paperback/ Hardcover	Specific Edition *If Applicable*	Quantity

SHIPPING INFORMATION

Contact:

Title:

School/District:

Address Line 1:

Address Line 2:

Zip or Postal Code:

Phone:

Mobile:

Email:

BILLING INFORMATION ☐ *SAME AS SHIPPING*

Contact:

Title:

School/District:

Address Line 1:

Address Line 2:

Zip or Postal Code:

Phone:

Mobile:

Email:

PAYMENT INFORMATION

☐ CREDIT CARD

Name on Card:

Card Number:

Expiration Date:

Security Code:

☐ PO

Purchase Order Number:

StudySync Text Fulfillment, BookheadEd Learning, LLC
610 Daniel Young Drive | Sonoma, CA 95476